Small Plates

Small Plates
Appetizers as Meals

Marguerite Marceau Henderson

Gibbs Smith, Publisher
Salt Lake City

First Edition
10 09 08   5 4

Published by
Gibbs Smith, Publisher
P.O. Box 667
Layton, Utah 84041

Orders: 1.800.748.5439
www.gibbs-smith.com

Designed by Deibra McQuiston
Printed and bound in Hong Kong

Library of Congress Cataloging-in-Publication Data

Henderson, Marguerite Marceau.
  Small plates : appetizers as meals / Marguerite Marceau Henderson ; photographs
by Adam Finkle.— 1st ed.
     p. cm.
  ISBN 10:1-58685-781-9 ISBN 13:978-1-58685-781-3
  1. Appetizers. 2. Cookery, International. I. Title.

TX740.H465 2006
641.8'1—dc22

2005025784

Contents

Acknowledgments

There are never enough lines in a book to thank all who have contributed to my career, as well as to my writing of this book.

First and foremost, I always attribute my love of cooking to my late mother, Rose Filippi Marceau, to whom my first cookbook, *Savor the Memories,* was dedicated. It was her love of food, and of its preparation and serving, that instilled in me a passion for all that is delicious. She was a true pioneer in the art of serving freshly prepared meals every evening, using her Sicilian culinary skills and her sense of adventure in the kitchen. She prepared exotic and always triumphant dishes. She was an icon in our family, and to this day the fortunate diners at her abundant table recall Rose's enthusiasm for entertaining, her impeccable table setting, her lavish dishes, and her effervescent smile.

I would like to thank the citizens of Utah, who have embraced my Mediterranean style of cooking. They are receptive to new ideas, and this is fertile ground for planting the seed of creating freshly prepared dishes daily. They have taken my cooking classes for over a quarter of a century—some students are perennial attendees—bought my cookbook, eaten at my former deli, Cucina, and have faithfully watched my cooking segment every Wednesday at noon on KSL Channel 5 for over five years.

Thanks also go to the fine purveyors of Salt Lake City, who have introduced the populace to a laundry list of ingredients once only a wish, but now a reality. We are now able to acquire radicchio, arugula, heirloom tomatoes, French imported cheeses, California black mission figs and baby artichokes, and first cold pressed Sicilian olive oil. Artisan breads and cheeses are locally produced, along with tender lamb from Morgan Valley Lamb, and some of the best organic produce, fruits, and vegetables are showcased at the summer farmers markets in the area.

Thanks to Nancy Beykirch, owner of Love to Cook at Kitchen Kneads in Logan, Utah. She opened the doors to cooking students of Cache Valley for my classes for years, and I am most grateful.

I couldn't have written or even thought about writing a second book without the assistance of Gibbs Smith, Publisher, who believes in up-and-coming local cookbook authors. Thanks.

And most of all, thanks to my dear family and friends who make cooking for them a joy. They know they will never leave my house hungry or thirsty, are always welcome to break bread, share a glass of wine, or just linger over a cup of coffee and a homemade scone.

Thanks to my son, Justin Churchill Henderson, who makes his mother proud every day as an attorney in the U.S. Navy. He has a talent in the kitchen, too—an inherited family trait—and makes a mean veal scallopini with wild mushrooms. And he is a beautiful and thoughtful writer.

Thanks to my daughter, Sarah Henderson Collins, and her husband, Sean, who are both wizards in the kitchen; he makes the pasta, she bakes the cookies. They make me burst with pride with their scholarly accomplishments—Sarah's M.B.A. and Sean's studies at Creighton University Medical School.

Thanks even to my ex-husband, Robert Hill Henderson, who can clean up a kitchen with one hand tied behind his back and wash more dishes at holidays than anyone!

Thanks to my immediate family from New York—they are still my biggest fans, especially my brother, George, and my cousins, Maria, Lisa, Anita, and Michael. Grazie!

And thanks to Adam Finkle, the most patient food photographer in Salt Lake City, who made the shoot as smooth as possible; Susan Massey, food stylist extraordinaire for her contribution of countless hours of expertise; Mary Schwing and Kristen Hopson, my kitchen assistants for years, especially during the grueling hours of the photo shoot; and of course to all my loyal friends who have been there for me for decades—Ellen Hutchinson, Amelia Rosene, Krista Stoker, Eileen Mullane, Kelly Fisher, Patty Hoagland, Karen Boe, Virginia Rainey, Pollyanna Pixton, and all others who have supported the noble cause of fine food and wine.

Buon Appetito!

Introduction

What are "small plates"? They are unpretentious bites of robust and intense flavors, more substantial than a cocktail snack, but not as hearty as an entrée. They are ideal for diners who are curious about flavor, adventurous about taste, and who want to vary their dining experience as much as possible in one sitting. Small plates are a relaxed style of entertaining and dining. There is no stress in trying to get all the courses on the table at the same time because they are served as prepared. Guests also enjoy appropriate pours of wines to complement the dishes.

If time, budget, and dietary issues are fundamental, then small plates are the perfect solution. Each recipe keeps time in the kitchen to a minimum, allowing the cook to select two or three recipes for diners to share family style. No expensive cuts of meat, no *foie gras* or caviar for exclusive palates, and no nutritional requirements that cannot be met. Small plates also easily allow your attractive serving platters—whether family heirloom fine china or tag-sale finds—to enhance presentation.

The small plate concept is not new. It is the foundation of many European and Asian menus: small portions of an assortment of dishes. The Italians have *antipasti*, the Chinese have *dim sum*, and the Spanish have *tapas*. The small plate is the way I love to eat when given the choice at a restaurant. Why order an entrée of just two or three textures

and tastes when, for the same price and amount of food, you can have an array of dishes and experience a multitude of flavors? Countless times I've perused the appetizer or starter menu and found the selections much more intriguing than the pricier and larger entrées. And when I travel, whether abroad or just to the next county, I try to sample as much of the local cuisine as possible. A few samples from the appetizer menu give me a culinary sense of the area.

It's hard not to be nostalgic about traveling to the Pacific Northwest where I had a bowl of steamed Penn Cove mussels in shallot-butter broth and a salad of mixed greens with lightly toasted hazelnuts and Oregon bleu cheese. And, of course, I can't pass up any crab cake chock-full of fresh Dungeness crabmeat, usually served with an original aioli, without thinking of the region. In Sicily, I had one dinner that included warmed bruschetta with wild mushrooms and regional cheeses, *pasta alla Norma* (bucatini with grilled sardines), and a plate of freshly grilled seasonal vegetables (eggplant, squash, fennel, and onions). A memorable meal from Greece was spit-grilled lamb chops with fresh oregano, a burst of squeezed lemon, and a tangy yogurt mint sauce—my small plate included a half-serving of those lamb chops with a salad of feta, kalamata olives, ruby-red tomatoes, and cucumber. It was ideal for sharing with fellow diners, each of whom also had ordered small plates to pass around. All of these memorable meals were comprised of small portions of signature foods with unique flavors.

Small Plates: Appetizers as Meals is a compilation of recipes—many inspired by my travels in the Mediterranean, all tested scores of times in my kitchen—that have sustained me over years of entertaining, teaching cooking classes, television appearances, and family dinners. They are a guideline; deviate according to your specific tastes and desires.

This book is designed to help you create an assembly of dishes that are perfect for sharing or entertaining. This cookbook was inspired by a series of classes I taught for several years titled "Appetizers as Meals." The classes were an overwhelming success. Students clamored for more easy entertaining ideas involving minimal fuss for parties and informal dinners.

Plan a small plates buffet for your next party to include five or six simply prepared dishes, many of which can be done hours in advance. When creating a menu, consider colors and textures of the foods, ease in serving, and variety of vegetable, poultry, meat, and seafood for guests who might have dietary restrictions. You'll find everything you need in the pages of this book.

Recently, I hosted a summer party for thirty guests on my patio under the grapevine-covered pergola. I had a selection of Mozzarella, Tomato, and Prosciutto Bruschetta, using freshly picked garden heirloom tomatoes (see page 24), Asian Grilled Steak on Sesame Slaw, for the carnivores (see page 52), Paparadelle alla Primavera—lots of fresh vegetables for the nonmeat eaters (see page 91), Cajun Shrimp and Andouille Salad, for the not so faint of heart (see page 109), and a Fresh Fig and Gorgonzola Crostada, to showcase the season's fresh black mission figs (I used figs instead of pears, see page 38). The menu reflected the bounty of a late-summer harvest. It was a hit with the party-goers, evident by the empty platters at the end of the evening. Everyone was satiated; no one had overindulged.

Preparation was less than four hours. Serving involved merely placing several abundantly filled small platters—perfect for displaying the final product—on the outdoor dining table and having guests replenish their plates with a selection customized for their palates and appetites.

So retrieve those precious small dishes from dusty closets and shelves, fill them with morsels of shrimp, chicken, vegetables, rice, pasta, or salad. Then invite fortunate friends to experience the joy of your small plates. Pepper the table with lively conversation and pour a few glasses of fine wine. A complete dining experience is in the making.

Breadstuffs

THE RECIPES

Cheese and Herb Batons

Individual Cheese Soufflés

Mozzarella, Tomato, and Prosciutto Bruschetta

Christmas Morning Chicken and Artichoke Strata

Cranberry-Ginger Stuffed Brie

Curried Scallops in Puff Pastry Shells

Grilled Pizza Margherita

Muffuleta (New Orleans Italian Sandwich)

Pancetta and White Beans Crostini

Pancetta, Caramelized Onion, and Brie Tarts

Shrimp Salad Bruschetta

Smoked Salmon and Asparagus Bundles

Prosciutto and Cheese Turnovers

Cheese, Herb, and Ham Pastries

Nutty Caramel Baked Brie

Pear and Gorgonzola Crostada

Wild Mushroom and Fontina Bruschetta

Arugula, Prosciutto, and Pears Crostini

Warm Mozzarella and Tomato Bruschetta

Tourtiere (Meat Pie)

Italian Sausage Pinwheels

All-Purpose Piecrust

Tomato and Olive Tart

Portobello Mushroom Turnovers

Shiitake, Fennel, and Ricotta Bruschetta

Cheese and Herb Batons

1 package (17.3 ounces) frozen puff
 pastry sheets, thawed
2 tablespoons melted butter
1 cup shredded Parmesan or Romano
 cheese
1 cup crumbled blue cheese or
 Gorgonzola
2 tablespoons dried Italian seasoning

MAKES 15 SERVINGS (2 EACH)

Place the two thawed pastry sheets on work surface. Brush both with melted butter.

In a bowl, combine the shredded Parmesan or Romano cheese and crumbled blue cheese. Stir in the dried Italian seasoning. Spread the cheese mixture evenly on bottom half of each pastry sheet, then fold the top half of pastry over the filling to form an "envelope," press the pastry down slightly to flatten and the seal the edges to secure filling. Cut each "envelope" into 1/2-inch-wide strips, twist each strip three or four times and place each twist on a parchment paper or Silpat lined baking sheet. Bake in preheated oven at 425 degrees F for 12 to 15 minutes on middle shelf until golden brown. Serve with salads, an appetizer with cocktails, or as an afternoon snack.

Individual Cheese Soufflés

6 large eggs, separated
³/₄ cup half-and-half
¹/₂ teaspoon salt
¹/₈ teaspoon ground white pepper
Pinch cayenne pepper
¹/₂ cup grated Parmesan or Romano
 cheese
1 cup shredded Manchego cheese or
 white cheddar cheese
2 cups soft bread cut into 1/2-inch
 cubes (use bread without crusts)

MAKES 6 SERVINGS

In a medium bowl, beat egg yolks, half-and-half, salt, white pepper, and cayenne pepper. Add cheeses and bread cubes. Let rest for at least 30 minutes to allow the bread to soak up the egg mixture.

Beat egg whites until stiff peaks form. Fold into egg and bread mixture. Butter six 8-ounce ramekins. Pour the mixture into ramekins and place the ramekins in a deep baking pan with hot water filled half way up the sides of the ramekins to make a *bain-marie*. Bake in a preheated oven at 375 degrees F for 25 minutes, or until puffed and golden. Times might vary slightly. Souffles are done when a toothpick inserted in the center comes out clean. Serve immediately.

Cheese and Herb Batons

Mozzarella, Tomato, and Prosciutto Bruschetta

BRUSCHETTA

1   loaf Italian bread

Olive oil

TOPPING

1   container (16 ounces) bocconcini (bite-sized mozzarella balls), drained or 1 pound fresh mozzarella, cut into 1/2-inch cubes

1   pound grape tomatoes or pear-shaped baby tomatoes, cut in half lengthwise

1   clove garlic, minced

1/4   cup extra virgin olive oil

1/8   teaspoon red pepper flakes

4   paper thin slices prosciutto, cut into 1/4-inch-wide strips

1/4   cup chopped sun dried tomatoes in olive oil

1/2   cup chopped roasted red peppers

2   tablespoons chopped fresh parsley

2   tablespoons chopped fresh basil

1/2   teaspoon kosher salt

MAKES 6 SERVINGS (2 EACH)

To make bruschetta, cut the bread into 1-inch-thick slices on the diagonal to make about 12 slices. Brush with olive oil, and then toast in the oven in single layer for 10 minutes at 375 degrees F or grill on an outdoor grill.

In a medium bowl, combine the mozzarella, tomatoes, garlic, oil, red pepper flakes, prosciutto, sun dried tomatoes, red peppers, parsley, basil, and salt. Toss gently to combine. The recipe can be made several hours ahead up to this point. Place the toasted slices of bread on a serving platter. Top each slice with some of the mozzarella mixture. Drizzle lightly with more olive oil, if desired.

Christmas Morning Chicken and Artichoke Strata

BREAD AND EGG MIXTURE

12	large eggs
2	cups half-and-half
1	tablespoon dried Italian seasoning
1	teaspoon paprika
2	teaspoons kosher salt
1	teaspoon ground black pepper
1	loaf (1 1/2 pounds) soft Italian or French bread, cut into 1-inch cubes

CHICKEN AND ARTICHOKE MIXTURE

2	tablespoons butter
1	small onion, chopped
1	pound boneless and skinless chicken breasts, cut into 1-inch pieces
1	cup sliced mushrooms
1	can (15 ounces) artichoke hearts, coarsely chopped
1	red pepper, cored and diced
1/2	cup chopped fresh parsley
1	cup grated Romano or Parmesan cheese

TOPPING

8	ounces fresh mozzarella, thinly sliced
4	Roma tomatoes, coarsely chopped
1/2	cup chopped fresh basil

MAKES 12 SERVINGS

In a large bowl, beat the eggs, half-and-half, Italian seasoning, paprika, salt, and pepper. Toss in the cubed bread. Allow bread to soak for 10 to 15 minutes while preparing the remaining ingredients.

In a skillet, heat butter and sauté the onion until soft. Stir in the chicken; cook over medium heat until golden brown on all sides. Add the mushrooms. Cook for 5 more minutes. Stir in the artichoke hearts, red pepper, and parsley. Spray a 9 x 13 x 3-inch baking dish with vegetable spray or use ten 8-ounce individual ramekins. Toss the chicken mixture with the bread and eggs. Add the grated cheese and mix well. Pour into prepared dish or ramekins. Cover loosely with foil. Refrigerate overnight or for at least 2 hours.

Bake in preheated oven at 350 degrees F for 1 hour for the large pan or 30 minutes for the ramekins; remove foil. Top with sliced mozzarella and chopped tomatoes. Return to oven for 5 to 10 minutes for cheese to melt. Remove from oven; top with fresh basil. Cut into 12 pieces and serve at once.

Cranberry-Ginger Stuffed Brie

Cranberry-Ginger Stuffed Brie

1/2 cup canned whole cranberry sauce
or 1/2 cup apricot preserves

1 teaspoon pumpkin pie spice

1/4 cup chopped walnuts, pecans,
almonds, or hazelnuts

1 teaspoon grated fresh gingerroot

8 ounces wheel brie or camembert,
placed in the freezer for 10 minutes
before using

1 sheet (from 17.3-ounce package)
frozen puff pastry sheets, thawed

1 egg, beaten

1 tablespoon cream

MAKES 4 SERVINGS

In a small bowl, combine the cranberry sauce
or apricot preserves, pumpkin pie spice, nuts, and
ginger. Cut the wheel of brie or camembert in half
horizontally and place on work surface cut sides
up. Spread the cranberry mixture over one half of
the cheese. Top with remaining half, cut side
down, sandwich-style. Place thawed sheet of puff
pastry on a work surface. Place the filled brie in
center of sheet, and then fold up the sides over
the cheese, securing the pastry to ensure there are
no exposed pieces of cheese. Turn the cheese-
filled pastry over so that the smooth surface is on
top and place it on a baking sheet lined with
parchment paper or Silpat.

Make an egg wash by beating together the
egg and cream. Brush cheese-filled pastry with
egg wash. Bake on middle shelf of preheated oven
at 425 degrees F for 20 minutes, until golden
brown. Cool for 10 to 15 minutes before slicing.
Serve with grapes, apple slices, pear slices, dried
apricots, dried dates, or thinly sliced French bread.

NOTE: This recipe can easily be doubled
using a 15 ounce wheel of cheese, doubling the
filling, and using two sheets of pastry, one for top
and another for bottom, cutting away excess.
Bake for an additional 5 minutes to ensure the filling is warmed.

Curried Scallops in Puff Pastry Shells

FILLING

4   tablespoons butter
1   small onion, diced
1   teaspoon curry powder
1/4   cup sherry or Madeira
1   cup heavy cream
2   teaspoons bottled chili sauce
2   tablespoons Major Grey's mango chutney
1/2   teaspoon kosher salt

PASTRY SHELLS

1   package frozen puff pastry shells (6 shells in each package)

SCALLOPS

1   pound large sea scallops, quartered and patted dry
1   cup flour
1/2   teaspoon kosher salt
1/8   teaspoon white pepper
4   tablespoons butter
1/2   cup white wine
1/4   cup toasted sliced or slivered almonds

MAKES 6 SERVINGS

In a medium skillet, heat the butter and sauté the onion until soft. Stir in the curry powder, cook 1 minute, and then add sherry, cream, chili sauce, mango chutney, and salt. Cook over low heat until thickened slightly. Set aside. This can be made several hours ahead, and then refrigerated until ready to use.

Bake the frozen puff pastry shells according to package directions. Remove any doughy part left in the center of the shells. Set shells aside.

Dredge the scallops in the flour mixed with salt and pepper. Heat a large skillet and add the butter. Sauté scallops in butter, stirring often; cook until opaque, about 2 minutes. Add wine and cook another minute. Add the curry sauce to scallops; cook for 1 minute until sauce is heated through. Place the pastry shells on a serving plate, place some of the filling in each one, sprinkle with almonds, and serve at once.

Curried Scallops in Puff Pastry Shells

Grilled Pizza Margherita

1   package pizza dough (in tube),
    rolled out into 2 (6-inch) circles*
2   tablespoons extra virgin olive oil
4   Roma tomatoes, thinly sliced
8   ounces mozzarella, thinly sliced or
    shredded
1/2   cup chopped fresh basil
1   teaspoon kosher salt
1/2   cup shaved Parmesan cheese
Freshly ground black pepper to taste

MAKES 8 SERVINGS

Heat an outdoor grill on low. Brush the dough on both sides with olive oil. Place on grill and cook for 2 minutes. Turn the dough, top with tomatoes, mozzarella, basil, salt, and pepper. Cover grill; bake for 8 to 10 minutes or until dough has risen slightly and is golden brown. Top with shaved Parmesan cheese. Cut each pizza into 4 wedges and serve at once.

*You can use your own pizza dough recipe for 2 (6-inch) pizzas if you like.

Muffuleta (New Orleans Italian Sandwich)

ARTICHOKE RELISH

2   tablespoons olive oil
2   large cloves garlic, minced
1/2   teaspoon dried oregano
1   jar (16 ounces) mixed vegetables in
    vinegar, drained and coarsely
    chopped*
1   jar (8 ounces) marinated artichokes,
    drained and coarsely chopped
1/2   cup coarsely chopped roasted red
    peppers
1/4   cup coarsely chopped pimiento-
    stuffed green olives

SANDWICH

1   round (10-inch) loaf Italian bread
1/4   pound thinly sliced Black Forest ham
1/4   pound thinly sliced Genoa salami
1/4   pound sliced provolone
1/4   pound sliced mozzarella

MAKES 4 TO 6 SERVINGS

In a small skillet, heat oil. Add garlic and oregano; sauté for 1 minute on low heat. Remove from heat and place in a food processor with vegetables, artichokes, red peppers, and olives. Pulse on and off 3 to 4 times. Mixture should be blended, not pureed.

Cut the round of bread in half horizontally. Remove some of the bread from the center of the bottom half of the loaf to make a shallow well for the filling. Spread half the artichoke relish on bottom half of bread, then top with layers of ham, salami, and cheeses, alternating the meat and cheese layers. Spread the top half of the bread with remaining artichoke relish. Cover the meats and cheeses with top half of bread, press down, and wrap the sandwich in plastic wrap, then in foil. Refrigerate at least 2 hours and up to 24 hours to allow the flavors to meld. Cut into 4 to 6 wedges.

*Italian garden vegetables work well.

Grilled Pizza Margherita

Pancetta and White Beans Crostini

CROSTINI

1 French baguette
Olive oil

TOPPING

2 tablespoons olive oil
2 thin slices pancetta, chopped
2 tablespoons chopped sun dried tomatoes in olive oil
1 can (15 ounces) cannellini or great northern white beans, drained
1 large clove garlic, minced
1 tablespoon chopped fresh basil
$1/2$ teaspoon kosher salt
$1/4$ teaspoon ground black pepper
$1/4$ cup grated Romano cheese

MAKES 8 SERVINGS (2 EACH)

To make the crostini, cut the baguette into 1/2-inch-thick slices on the diagonal to make about 16 slices. Brush with a little olive oil and bake at 375 degrees F for 10 minutes, turning once to brown both sides.

In a skillet, heat oil and sauté pancetta until crispy. Add sun dried tomatoes, white beans, and garlic; cook another 2 to 3 minutes until beans are heated through. Add basil, salt, and pepper. Place 1 heaping tablespoon bean mixture on each toasted bread round and sprinkle with grated cheese. Serve at once.

Pancetta, Caramelized Onion, and Brie Tarts

1 sheet puff pastry (from a 17.3-ounce package), thawed and rolled out
$1/4$ pound pancetta or high-quality bacon, chopped
1 large sweet onion, such as Vidalia, Walla Walla, or Maui, chopped
1 teaspoon dried thyme leaves
$1/4$ pound brie, camembert, or other soft cheese, cut into small pieces
$1/4$ cup grated Romano or Parmesan cheese
$1/2$ teaspoon kosher salt
$1/4$ teaspoon ground black pepper

MAKES 4 SERVINGS

Place the rolled out sheet of puff pastry on a work surface. Cut into fourths. Crimp the edges of each square to form a 1/2-inch border all around each pastry. Place the pastries on a baking sheet lined with parchment paper or Silpat.

In a medium skillet, sauté the pancetta or bacon for 2 to 3 minutes. Add onion and thyme leaves; cook for 5 minutes on medium heat, until onion is golden. Remove from heat, stir in the cheeses, salt, and pepper. Divide the mixture among the 4 pastry squares. Bake at 425 degrees F for 25 minutes until pastry is golden and filling is melted. Cool slightly before serving.

Shrimp Salad Bruschetta

BRUSCHETTA

1   loaf Italian bread
Olive oil

TOPPING

1   pound large raw shrimp, peeled and deveined
$\frac{1}{4}$ teaspoon paprika
2   tablespoons olive oil
1   large clove garlic, minced
$\frac{1}{2}$ teaspoon kosher salt
4   Roma tomatoes, chopped
$\frac{1}{4}$ cup chopped fresh Italian parsley
2   tablespoons chopped fresh basil leaves
1   tablespoon capers
$\frac{1}{4}$ cup pimiento-stuffed Spanish olives, sliced
    Juice of 2 lemons
$\frac{1}{2}$ teaspoon kosher salt
$\frac{1}{4}$ cup extra virgin olive oil
1   cup grated Manchego or Monterey Jack cheese

To make bruschetta, cut the bread into 1-inch-thick slices on the diagonal to make about 12 slices. Brush with olive oil, and then toast in the oven in single layer for 10 minutes at 375 degrees F or grill on an outdoor grill.

In a medium bowl, combine the shrimp, paprika, oil, garlic, and salt. Toss. Marinate for 1 hour. Grill the shrimp on an outdoor grill, in a grill pan, or skillet for 2 to 3 minutes per side until pink.

Coarsely chop the shrimp and place in a bowl with chopped tomatoes, parsley, basil, capers, olives, lemon juice, salt, and oil. Place the bread slices on baking sheet, top each with some of the shrimp salad, and sprinkle on the grated cheese. Bake in a preheated oven at 400 degrees F for 3 minutes until cheese is melted and shrimp is heated through.

Smoked Salmon and Asparagus Bundles

Smoked Salmon and Asparagus Bundles

3	cups water
1	teaspoon kosher salt
1	teaspoon oil
24	spears asparagus, trimmed to 3-inch length with tips intact
12	sheets phyllo dough
½	cup butter, melted
6	ounces herbed cheese such as boursin or alouette
½	pound thinly sliced smoked salmon
1	egg, beaten
1	tablespoon cream
2	tablespoons black and white sesame seed combo or 2 tablespoons toasted sesame seeds

MAKES 12 SERVINGS (2 EACH)

Bring water to a boil in a medium-sized saucepan. Add salt and oil. Immerse trimmed asparagus spears in water, reduce heat to a simmer, and blanch the asparagus for 2 minutes until bright green. Drain. Cool to room temperature.

Place the 12 sheets of phyllo dough on the kitchen counter and cover with a damp dish towel. Place one sheet on a work surface, brush entirely with melted butter, top with a second sheet of phyllo, and brush with more butter. Cut the sheets lengthwise into 4 strips. Place a dollop of cheese about 2 inches up from bottom of each strip, and top each dollop with a small piece of smoked salmon and an asparagus spear, allowing 1 inch of the spear to extend past the strip of dough. Roll up each strip of phyllo from the bottom to the top, to form a cylinder. Place seam side down on a baking sheet lined with parchment paper or Silpat.

Repeat this process 6 times, using the remaining sheets of phyllo. You will have 24 bundles when you are finished. Be sure to keep the sheets covered with a damp dish towel while working. Make an egg wash by beating together the egg and cream. Brush each bundle with egg wash, sprinkle with sesame seeds, and bake at 375 degrees F for 12 to 15 minutes until golden brown. Serve warm.

Prosciutto and Cheese Turnovers

1   package (17.3 ounces) frozen puff pastry sheets, thawed
2   cups whole-milk ricotta cheese
1   cup shredded mozzarella
1/2   cup + 2 tablespoons grated Romano cheese, divided
1/2   pound prosciutto or Black Forest ham, diced
2   eggs
1/4   cup chopped fresh parsley
1   teaspoon kosher salt
1/4   teaspoon ground black pepper
1   tablespoon cream

MAKES 9 SERVINGS (2 EACH)

Place pastry dough on a lightly floured work surface and roll out to make each sheet a 9-inch square. Cut each pastry sheet into 3 strips by 3 strips, so you have 9 squares per sheet.

In a bowl, combine ricotta, mozzarella, 1/2 cup Romano cheese, prosciutto or ham, 1 egg, parsley, salt, and pepper. Mix well. Place a tablespoon of filling in center of each square. Fold into a triangle and crimp edges with a fork. Make an egg wash by beating together 1 egg with the cream. Brush each turnover with egg wash and sprinkle with remaining 2 tablespoons of grated cheese. Place turnovers on a baking sheet lined with parchment paper or Silpat. Preheat oven to 425 degrees F and bake turnovers for 12 to 15 minutes on middle shelf until golden and puffed. Serve warm.

Cheese, Herb, and Ham Pastries

1   package (17.3 ounces) frozen puff pastry sheets, thawed
2 to 3 tablespoons Dijon or any other dark coarse-grain mustard
1/4   cup combination chopped fresh herbs such as thyme, parsley, basil, chives, and tarragon
1/2   pound thinly sliced ham (such as Black Forest, prosciutto, or coppa)
1/2   pound sliced Swiss, provolone, or Havarti cheese
1   egg, beaten
1   tablespoon cream

MAKES 8 SERVINGS (3 EACH)

Lay one of the pastry sheets on a work surface. Spread with mustard, sprinkle on herbs, and then lay ham and cheese slices evenly on pastry, leaving 1/2-inch border on all sides. Top with second sheet of pastry and crimp edges. Make very light cuts on the diagonal about 1 inch apart on the pastry to form a diamond design. Make an egg wash by beating together the egg and cream. Brush pastry with egg wash and bake on a baking sheet lined with parchment paper or Silpat for 20 to 25 minutes at 425 degrees F until golden and puffed. Remove from oven; cool 10 minutes before cutting into 2-inch squares.

Nutty Caramel Baked Brie

1 package (17.3 ounces) frozen puff pastry sheets, thawed
1 wheel brie (15 ounces), placed in freezer for 15 minutes before using
$1/2$ cup chopped pecans or walnuts
$1/2$ cup packed brown sugar
$1/2$ teaspoon ground cinnamon
1 egg, beaten
1 tablespoon cream

MAKES 8 TO 10 SERVINGS

Place one sheet of pastry on a work surface. Cut the brie in half horizontally. In a bowl, mix the pecans or walnuts, brown sugar, and cinnamon. Spread the nut mixture evenly on the cut side of the bottom half of brie, then top with remaining half of brie, sandwich-style. Place brie on one sheet of puff pastry. Cut 1 inch off the corners of the pastry to form a rough circle, and then fold the pastry up the sides of the brie and top with second sheet of pastry. Cut away excess pastry along sides, and seal the edges well, making sure there are no openings where cheese might be exposed. The recipe can be made several hours ahead up to this point and refrigerated.

Make an egg wash by beating together the egg and cream. Brush top and sides of pastry with egg wash. Roll out excess pastry dough and cut out shapes to place on the top of brie for garnish. Place cheese-filled pastry on a baking sheet lined with parchment paper or Silpat. Bake in preheated oven at 425 degrees F for 20 to 25 minutes until golden brown and puffed. Remove from oven; allow to cool slightly before slicing.

NOTE: I like to serve this with sliced apples, pears, dried apricots, dates, grapes, and toasted hazelnuts.

Pear and Gorgonzola Crostada

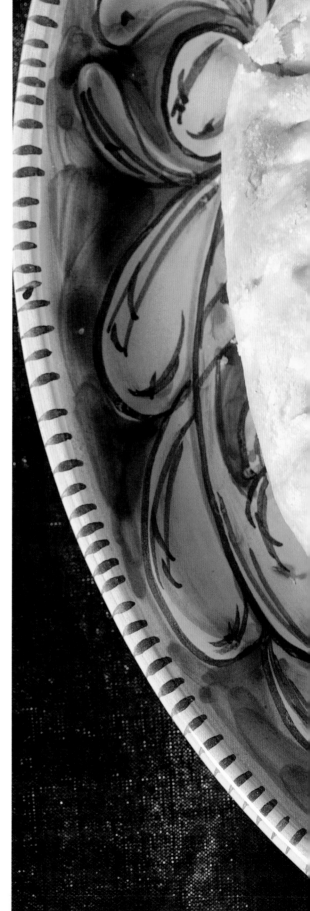

1   recipe All-Purpose Piecrust, made without the sugar (see page 45)
2   red onions, thinly sliced
2   tablespoons butter or olive oil
1   teaspoon kosher salt
3   D'Anjou or Comice pears*
1½   to 2 cups crumbled Gorgonzola cheese
½   cup almond slices, chopped walnuts, or pine nuts
2   tablespoons butter, cut into small pieces

MAKES 6 TO 8 SERVINGS

Roll out the piecrust pastry to a 14-inch diameter circle and place on a parchment-lined 14-inch round pizza pan. To make smaller crostadas, divide the dough in half and roll out each half to a 10-inch diameter circle; place each round of dough on a parchment-lined baking sheet.

Sauté the onions in butter or oil with salt for 8 to 10 minutes on low heat until soft and caramelized. Cool to room temperature. Cut the pears vertically into 1/8-inch thick slices, removing any seeds. Spread the onions on the pastry evenly, leaving a 1-inch border all around the pastry. Top each pastry with the thinly sliced pears, cut side up, in a single layer. Sprinkle on cheese and nuts, and dot with bits of butter.

Fold up the 1-inch border over the filling so there is a band of crust around the outer edge. Bake in a preheated oven at 425 degrees F on the middle shelf for 20 to 25 minutes until golden brown and the cheese is bubbly. Remove from oven and cool slightly before cutting into pieces.

*Pears may be substituted with 12 fresh large black mission figs, cut in half lengthwise.

NOTE: You can make this recipe with store-bought puff pastry sheets, thawed, or packaged piecrusts, in the same manner.

Pear and Gorgonzola Crostada

Wild Mushroom and Fontina Bruschetta

BRUSCHETTA

1   loaf Italian bread
Olive oil

TOPPING

2   tablespoons olive oil
1   medium onion, thinly sliced
2   cloves garlic, smashed
2   cups wild mushrooms
     (approximately), any combination
     (crimini, portobello, oyster, shiitake,
     chanterelles, porcini), thinly sliced
½   cup heavy cream
½   teaspoon kosher salt
¼   teaspoon ground black pepper
1   teaspoon dried thyme leaves
¼   pound fontina or other soft cheese
     (such as brie, goat cheese, or
     mozzarella), sliced

MAKES 6 SERVINGS (2 EACH)

To make bruschetta, cut the bread into 1-inch-thick slices on the diagonal to make about 12 slices. Brush with oil, and then toast in the oven in single layer for 10 minutes at 375 degrees F or grill on an outdoor grill. Place the toasted or grilled bread on a baking sheet in single layer.

In a medium skillet, heat olive oil and sauté onion until soft, about 3 to 4 minutes. Add garlic and mushrooms; cook 2 to 3 minutes until mushrooms are tender. Add cream, salt, pepper, and thyme. Cook on low heat for 2 minutes. Put equal amounts of the mixture on each of the bread rounds. Top each with cheese and bake in a preheated oven at 375 degrees F for 5 minutes just to warm through.

Arugula, Prosciutto, and Pears Crostini

CROSTINI

1   loaf French baguette
Olive oil

TOPPING

3 to 4 cups arugula leaves, coarsely
    chopped
8   very thin slices prosciutto, cut in half
    lengthwise to make 16 strips
3 to 4 D'Anjou or Bartlett pears, cored
    and thinly sliced (about 32 slices)
1   cup shaved Parmesan cheese
3 to 4 tablespoons olive oil*
Freshly ground black pepper

MAKES 8 SERVINGS (2 EACH)

To make the crostini, cut the baguette into 1/2-inch-thick slices on the diagonal to make about 16 slices. Brush with a little olive oil and bake at 375 degrees F for 10 minutes, turning once to brown both sides.

Place toasted slices of bread on a serving platter in single layer. Top each slice of bread with some arugula, 1 thin strip of prosciutto, 2 thin slices of pear, and then some shaved Parmesan. The recipe can be made an hour ahead up to this point. Before serving, drizzle with olive oil and grind some pepper on each.

*A teaspoon or two of truffle oil works beautifully, too!

Warm Mozzarella and Tomato Bruschetta

BRUSCHETTA

1   loaf Italian bread
Olive oil

TOPPING

2   cloves garlic, minced
1/3   cup balsamic vinegar
2/3   cup olive oil
2   shallots, minced
1   tablespoon capers
1   teaspoon kosher salt
1/4   teaspoon coarse ground black pepper
1/2   cup pitted kalamata olives, chopped
1/2   cup fresh basil leaves
8   Roma tomatoes
1   pound fresh mozzarella, cut into 16 slices

MAKES 8 SERVINGS (2 EACH)

To make bruschetta, cut bread into 1/2-inch-thick slices on the diagonal to make about 16 slices. Brush with olive oil, and then toast in the oven in single layer for 10 minutes at 375 degrees F or grill on an outdoor grill.

Place baguette slices in a single layer on a serving platter. In a bowl, combine the garlic, vinegar, oil, shallots, capers, salt, pepper, olives, and basil. Whisk well. Slice each of the tomatoes into 4 slices, lengthwise, to make 32 slices. Place a slice of tomato in a large baking dish, top with a slice of mozzarella, then top with another slice of tomato. Repeat this process until you have 16 tomato and mozzarella stacks. Drizzle each with some of the vinaigrette. The recipe can be made an hour ahead up to this point.

Place the baking dish in a preheated oven at 400 degrees F for 8 to 10 minutes, until cheese is melted. Remove from oven and place one tomato stack on each toasted bread round.

Warm Mozzarella and Tomato Bruschetta

Tourtiere (Meat Pie)

1   tablespoon vegetable oil
2   pounds ground pork
1   large onion, finely chopped
1   large russet potato, peeled and
    diced
2   cups button mushrooms, sliced
1   teaspoon kosher salt
1½ cups beef broth
½   teaspoon ground cinnamon
½   teaspoon coarsely ground black
    pepper
1   teaspoon dried savory or thyme
½   teaspoon ground cloves
1   cup fresh bread crumbs
½   cup chopped fresh Italian parsley
1   recipe All-Purpose Piecrust, made
    without the sugar (see page 45)
1   egg, beaten
1   tablespoon cream

MAKES 6 SERVINGS

In a large skillet, heat the vegetable oil and sauté the pork until no longer pink, crumbling as you cook. Add onion, potato, and mushrooms. Cook on medium heat for 5 minutes, stirring often. Add the salt, beef broth, cinnamon, pepper, savory or thyme, and cloves. Cover and simmer for 30 minutes. Stir in the bread crumbs and parsley. Taste for seasoning. Cool to room temperature before filling piecrust.

Place one of the piecrusts in a 9-inch pie pan, add meat filling, place second crust on top, and crimp edges. Beat egg with cream for egg wash and brush over top of pie. With a sharp knife, cut a diamond crisscross design on dough. Place pie on a baking sheet and bake at 375 degrees F for 30 to 35 minutes until crust is golden brown. Cool to room temperature before cutting into 6 wedges.

Italian Sausage Pinwheels

1 tablespoon olive oil
1 pound bulk Italian sausage (mild or sweet)
1 clove garlic, minced
¼ cup finely chopped Italian parsley
¼ cup finely chopped red bell pepper
1 tablespoon fennel seed
1 egg, beaten
1 package (17.3 ounces) frozen puff pastry sheets, thawed

MAKES 12 SERVINGS (2 EACH)

In a medium skillet, heat oil and sauté the sausage and garlic until sausage is browned, crumbling as you cook. Cool to room temperature and stir in the parsley, red pepper, fennel seed, and beaten egg. Roll out the 2 sheets of puff pastry. Place the sausage stuffing on each of the sheets in a thin layer. Roll up each sheet, jelly roll style, and secure the seams. The recipe can be refrigerated several hours at this point, wrapped in plastic wrap. With seam side down, cut each of the rolls into 12 pieces using a serrated knife. Place cut sides up on a baking sheet lined with parchment paper or Silpat and bake at 425 degrees F for 15 to 20 minutes until golden and puffed.

NOTE: Can be served at room temperature.

All-Purpose Piecrust

2 cups all-purpose flour
½ cup cold butter, cut into small pieces
½ cup cold shortening, cut into small pieces
1 teaspoon kosher salt
1 tablespoon sugar (if using a sweet filling)
¼ to ½ cup ice water

MAKES 2 (9-INCH) CRUSTS

In the work bowl of food processor or in a mixing bowl, combine flour, butter, shortening, salt, and sugar if using. Pulse on and off if using a metal blade, or cut in if using a pastry cutter, until butter and shortening are the size of peas. Add enough ice water, a few tablespoons at time, until the dough is soft, but not wet, when pressed together. Divide the dough in half, form a ball with each half, wrap in plastic, and then refrigerate until ready to use.

Tomato and Olive Tart

Tomato and Olive Tart

1   recipe All-Purpose Piecrust, made without the sugar (see page 45)
1   medium onion, thinly sliced
1   tablespoon extra virgin olive oil
4   large Roma tomatoes
¼   cup pitted kalamata olives
4   large eggs
1   cup half-and-half
4   ounces goat cheese, cut into small pieces
1   teaspoon dried herbs de Provence
1   teaspoon kosher salt
¼   teaspoon ground black pepper
½   cup grated Romano, Parmesan, or Asiago cheese
¼   cup chopped fresh Italian parsley

MAKES 6 SERVINGS

Place pastry in a 10-inch removable-bottom tart pan. Make sure the sides are not hanging over, but turned inside.

Sauté the onion in olive oil for 3 to 4 minutes until soft. Slice the tomatoes 1/4 inch thick. Place on paper towels to extract any excess liquid, then line bottom of tart pan with tomatoes. Top with sautéed onion and the olives.

In a medium bowl, beat the eggs, half-and-half, goat cheese, herbs de Provence, salt, and pepper. Pour into tart pan; top with grated cheese. Put the tart pan on a baking sheet to prevent spills in the oven and to make it easier to remove pan from oven. Bake in a preheated oven at 400 degrees F for 25 to 30 minutes until crust is golden and custard is set. Remove the tart from outer ring of tart pan, cool slightly, top with chopped parsley, and cut into 6 wedges.

Portobello Mushroom Turnovers

1 package (17.3 ounces) frozen puff pastry sheets, thawed
2 tablespoons butter
2 large shallots, chopped
2 large portobello mushrooms, caps only
1 teaspoon dried thyme leaves or 1 tablespoon fresh thyme leaves
1 teaspoon kosher salt
¼ teaspoon ground black pepper
1 cup grated Parmesan cheese, divided
2 large eggs
1 tablespoon cream

Place pastry dough on a lightly floured work surface and roll out to make each sheet a 9-inch square. Cut each pastry sheet into 3 strips by 3 strips, so you have 9 squares per sheet. In a medium skillet, heat butter and sauté shallots until soft and lightly golden. Coarsely chop mushrooms and add to pan along with thyme, salt, and pepper. Cook until mushrooms are softened, about 2 minutes. Place mushroom mixture in a food processor and pulse on and off until chopped, not pureed. Place mushroom mixture in a bowl, add half of the cheese and 1 egg; mix well.

Place a heaping tablespoon of filling in the center of each pastry square. Fold into a triangle and crimp edges with a fork. Place pastries on a baking sheet lined with parchment paper or Silpat. Make an egg wash by beating together 1 egg and the cream. Brush each turnover with egg wash and sprinkle with remaining Parmesan cheese.

Preheat oven to 425 degrees F and bake turnovers for 12 to 15 minutes on middle shelf until golden and puffed. Serve warm.

Shiitake, Fennel, and Ricotta Bruschetta

BRUSCHETTA

1   loaf Italian bread
Olive oil

TOPPING

2   tablespoons olive oil
2   tablespoons butter
2   cloves garlic, minced
4   cups fresh shiitake mushrooms, stems removed, thinly sliced
1   bulb fresh fennel, outer layer removed, thinly sliced
8   cups spinach leaves
1   teaspoon salt
$^{1}/_{2}$ teaspoon freshly ground black pepper
1   cup fresh ricotta cheese
1   cup grated Parmesan or Romano cheese
Olive oil for drizzling

To make bruschetta, cut the bread into 1-inch-thick slices on the diagonal to make about 12 slices. Brush with olive oil, and then toast in the oven in a single layer for 10 minutes at 375 degrees F or grill on an outdoor grill. Place the toasted or grilled bread on a baking sheet in single layer.

In a skillet, heat the oil and butter. Sauté garlic for 30 seconds. Add mushrooms and fennel; cook for 2 to 3 minutes until mushrooms are tender. Add spinach, salt, and pepper. Cover pan. Cook on high heat until spinach wilts, about 1 minute. Remove from pan. Place a heaping tablespoon of the spinach mixture on each slice of bread. Put a dollop of ricotta on each, then drizzle with a little oil and sprinkle with grated cheese. Place in a preheated oven at 375 degrees F for 5 to 7 minutes, until cheese is warmed and melted. Remove from oven and serve at once.

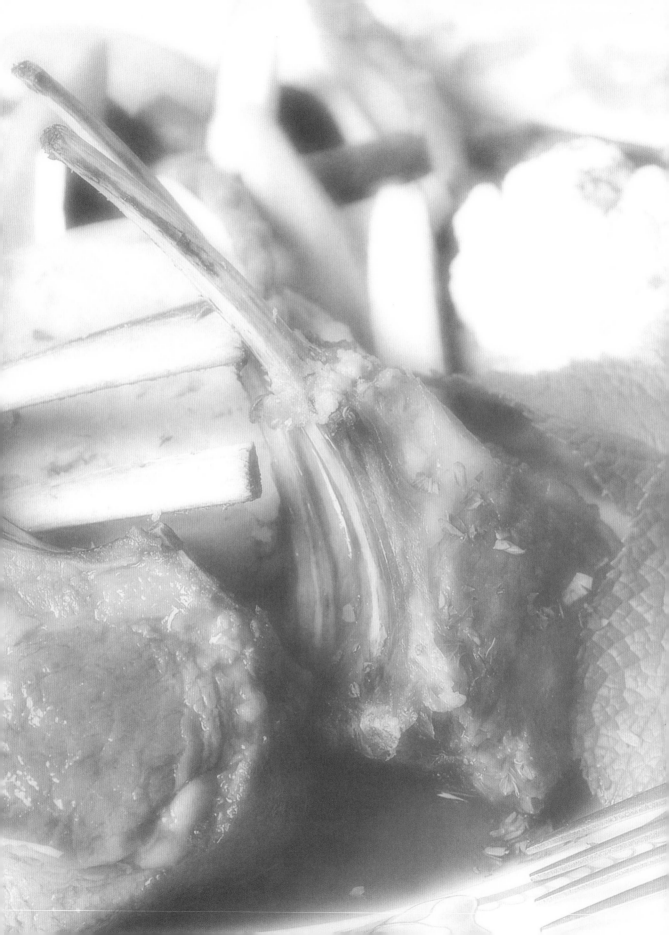

Meats and Poultry

THE RECIPES

Asian Grilled Steak on Sesame Slaw

SESAME SLAW

½ head green cabbage, thinly sliced
½ head red cabbage, thinly sliced
½ red onion, finely chopped
1 large carrot, peeled and shredded
½ pound fresh bean sprouts

DRESSING

¼ cup canola oil
2 tablespoons rice wine vinegar
2 tablespoons sugar
1 tablespoon sesame oil
¼ cup toasted sesame seeds
1 teaspoon kosher salt
1 large clove garlic, minced

STEAK

3 pounds tri-tip steak
¼ cup soy sauce
1 tablespoon Chinese Five Spice seasoning
2 tablespoons vegetable oil
2 large cloves garlic, minced
2 tablespoons sesame oil
1 tablespoon brown sugar
Juice and zest of 1 large orange
1 tablespoon minced fresh ginger
1 bunch green onions, thinly sliced on diagonal

MAKES 6 TO 8 SERVINGS

In a large mixing bowl, combine cabbages, red onion, carrot, and bean sprouts. Whisk all ingredients together for the dressing and toss into slaw. Refrigerate slaw at least 1 hour before serving. Recipe makes 8 cups of slaw.

Place steak in a glass or ceramic shallow pan. In a small bowl, combine soy sauce, Chinese Five Spice seasoning, vegetable oil, garlic, sesame oil, brown sugar, orange juice and zest, ginger, and green onions, whisking well. Pour over steaks; marinate for at least 2 hours in refrigerator, covered. Heat an outdoor grill to medium and cook steaks for 8 to 10 minutes per side, depending on thickness. The internal temperature should be about 120 degrees F for rare, 130 to 135 degrees F for medium. Remove from grill; allow to rest 5 minutes before slicing across the grain into thin slices. Discard the marinade. Serve steak over Sesame Slaw.

Asian Grilled Steak on Sesame Slaw

Beef and Vegetable Samosas

FILLING

4 medium new potatoes, cut into 1/2-inch dice

1 tablespoon fennel seeds

1 tablespoon ground cumin

1/2 teaspoon turmeric

1/4 cup vegetable oil

1 onion, chopped

1/4 serrano chile, cored and finely chopped*

1 piece (2 inches) fresh ginger, grated

3 large cloves garlic, minced

1/2 pound ground beef

2 cups green peas

1 teaspoon kosher salt

1/4 teaspoon black pepper

WRAPPERS

3 to 4 cups vegetable oil

1 package large wonton wrappers (about 5 x 5 inches)

1 egg, beaten

GARNISH

1 bottle (8 ounces) Major Grey's mango chutney

Cook potatoes in salted water until barely tender, about 15 minutes. Drain and cool. Place in mixing bowl. In a heavy dry skillet, heat the fennel seeds, cumin, and turmeric. Cook over medium heat for about 2 minutes, stirring often, until spices are darker in color and fragrant. Add oil, onion, chile, ginger, garlic, and beef. Cook over medium heat until beef is no longer pink. Stir in peas. Cook another minute; season with salt and pepper. Place mixture in bowl with potatoes; stir well and let cool. The recipe can be made a day ahead up to this point.

Place a wonton wrapper on a work surface and fill with about 2 tablespoons filling. Fold over into a triangle and seal with beaten egg. Repeat until you have used all the wonton wrappers. Heat 2 inches of vegetable oil in deep saucepan or fryer. Fry the turnovers one at a time in hot oil for 2 to 4 minutes until golden brown; remove with a slotted spoon to a plate lined with paper towels. Serve at once, with chutney if desired.

*You can add more serrano chile if a hotter filling is desired.

Beef Tenderloin Kebobs with Roquefort-Rosemary Sauce

BEEF

2   pounds beef tenderloin, cut into 1-inch pieces
2   tablespoons olive oil
2   cloves garlic, minced
1   teaspoon prepared horseradish
1   teaspoon Dijon mustard
1   cup full-bodied red wine
2   tablespoons finely chopped fresh rosemary
1   teaspoon coarse ground black pepper
12   (8-inch) wooden or metal skewers

ROQUEFORT-ROSEMARY SAUCE

1   cup crumbled Roquefort, blue, or Gorgonzola cheese
1   cup sour cream
½   cup heavy cream
4   sprigs or ¼ cup rosemary leaves
1   tablespoon prepared horseradish

MAKES 12 KEBOBS

Place the beef tenderloin pieces in a bowl with oil, garlic, horseradish, mustard, red wine, rosemary, and pepper. Marinate in refrigerator for 1 hour. Thread 3 to 4 pieces of the marinated beef on each skewer. (If you are using wooden skewers, soak in water for 10 minutes before threading to avoid burning on the grill.) Grill beef skewers over medium heat on an outdoor grill for 8 to 10 minutes, turning once, or roast in a preheated oven at 375 degrees F for 8 to 10 minutes, turning once. Serve with Roquefort-Rosemary Sauce.

To make the Roquefort-Rosemary Sauce, in a food processor or blender, combine cheese, sour cream, heavy cream, rosemary, and horseradish. Pulse on and off until smooth, about 30 seconds. This can be made a day ahead.

NOTE: This is great when served with Parslied Potatoes and Parsnips Parmesan (see page 184).

Chicken Piccata Brochettes

4 boneless and skinless chicken breast halves
2 cloves garlic, minced
2 tablespoons olive oil
Zest and juice of 1 lemon
1 teaspoon kosher salt
½ teaspoon ground black pepper
2 bay leaves
¼ cup chopped fresh sage
¼ cup chopped fresh rosemary
1 teaspoon dried thyme leaves
2 teaspoons capers
12 to 16 (10-inch) wooden skewers

MAKES 12 TO 16 BROCHETTES

Cut the chicken breasts into 1-inch pieces. Place in bowl along with garlic, oil, lemon zest and juice, salt, pepper, bay leaves, sage, rosemary, thyme, and capers. Toss; refrigerate for up to 6 hours. Remove the bay leaves. Soak wooden skewers in water for 10 minutes. Thread 4 to 5 pieces of chicken on each skewer, place on baking sheet, and top with the remaining marinade. Bake at 400 degrees F for 8 to 10 minutes. Serve warm.

Chicken Piccata Brochettes

Coconut Curry Chicken

CURRY SAUCE

3	tablespoons vegetable oil
1	large sweet onion, finely chopped
1	tablespoon grated fresh ginger
4	large cloves garlic, minced
3	tablespoons curry powder
1/2	teaspoon turmeric
1	teaspoon ground cumin
1/2	teaspoon ground cinnamon
2	tablespoons all-purpose flour
1	cup plain yogurt
3	tablespoons tomato paste
3	cups chicken broth

COCONUT CHICKEN

2	tablespoons vegetable oil
2	pounds boneless and skinless chicken breasts, cut into 1-inch pieces
2	cups frozen peas, thawed
1/2	cup sour cream
1	cup canned, unsweetened coconut milk
1/2	teaspoon kosher salt
1/2	teaspoon ground black pepper

OPTIONAL GARNISHES

Fresh cilantro sprigs

1	cup Major Grey's mango chutney
1	cup sliced bananas
1	cup chopped fresh mango
1/2	cup shredded unsweetened coconut
1	cup chopped toasted peanuts

MAKES 4 SERVINGS

In a medium saucepan, heat oil; add onion and cook on low heat for 3 to 5 minutes until softened. Add ginger, garlic, curry powder, turmeric, cumin, and cinnamon. Sauté for 2 to 3 minutes until fragrant. Stir in the flour. Cook 1 minute. Add the yogurt, tomato paste, and broth. Cover and simmer, whisking occasionally until thickened. The recipe can be made up to a day ahead to this point.

In a medium skillet, heat the vegetable oil and sauté the chicken pieces for 4 to 5 minutes until golden brown on all sides, but not necessarily cooked all the way through. Add the prepared Curry Sauce, cover, and simmer for 10 minutes. Stir in the peas, sour cream, and coconut milk and season with salt and pepper. Cook for 3 minutes on low heat. Do not boil! Transfer to a serving bowl and garnish with ingredients of choice.

Coffee and Spice Lamb Kebobs

COFFEE AND SPICE RUB

½ cup coarsely ground coffee beans
2 teaspoons ground cinnamon
1 teaspoon ground cumin
1 teaspoon ground allspice
1 tablespoon fennel seeds
2 cloves garlic, minced
1 teaspoon kosher salt
½ teaspoon coarsely ground black pepper
2 tablespoons olive oil
Zest and juice of 1 lemon

LAMB

2½ to 3 pounds boneless leg of lamb, trimmed of fat, cut into 1½-inch cubes
20 to 24 (6-inch) wooden or metal skewers
Lemon Mint Rice (see page 92)

MAKES 20 TO 24 KEBOBS

In a medium bowl, combine all ingredients for Coffee and Spice Rub. Add the cubed lamb pieces and toss well. Marinate in refrigerator for at least 30 minutes, and up to 2 hours.

If you are using wooden skewers, soak in water for 10 minutes. Thread 2 or 3 pieces of lamb onto the skewers. Place in a roasting pan or prepare an outdoor grill. Roast in a preheated oven at 350 degrees F for 8 to 10 minutes, or grill over medium heat for 3 to 4 minutes per side. Lamb should be pink in center, not overcooked. Serve over Lemon Mint Rice.

Holiday Spiced Game Hens

Holiday Spiced Game Hens

Zest and juice of 1 large orange

2   cups pomegranate or cranberry juice

1   cup honey

1   teaspoon ground coriander

1   teaspoon ground cinnamon

1   teaspoon ground allspice

¼   teaspoon cayenne pepper

4 to 6 large cloves garlic, smashed

1   teaspoon kosher salt

½   teaspoon ground black pepper

4   game hens, cut in half through the breastbone

Seeds of 1 pomegranate (for garnish)

1   cup chopped nuts of choice (for garnish)

MAKES 4 SERVINGS

In a medium bowl, combine the orange zest and juice, pomegranate or cranberry juice, honey, coriander, cinnamon, allspice, cayenne pepper, garlic, salt, and pepper; stir well. Divide mixture in half; marinate the hens in one half of the liquid for 1 to 8 hours. Drain off the marinade and discard; roast the hens, skin side up, for 25 to 30 minutes at 350 degrees F. In a small pan, heat the remaining half of marinade until thickened slightly. When hens are done roasting, drizzle with thickened sauce, sprinkle with pomegranate seeds and nuts, and serve at once.

Lamb Riblets with Minty Red Wine Sauce

LAMB RIBLETS

2 racks of lamb, cut into individual chops to make about 16 chops

¼ cup balsamic vinegar

2 tablespoons extra virgin olive oil

2 cloves garlic, minced

1 tablespoon fennel seeds

1 teaspoon kosher salt

1 teaspoon ground cinnamon

1 teaspoon dried oregano

1 teaspoon coarse ground black pepper

MINTY RED WINE SAUCE

2 tablespoons butter

2 shallots, peeled and chopped

1¼ cups dry red wine or beef broth, divided

1 teaspoon cornstarch

1 teaspoon ground allspice

¼ cup currant jelly

½ cup chopped fresh mint leaves

MAKES 4 SERVINGS (4 EACH)

"French" the bones by trimming fat and meat from bones to form "handles" on each chop. Place the chops in a ceramic or glass shallow pan. In a small bowl, combine the vinegar, oil, garlic, fennel, salt, cinnamon, oregano, and pepper. Pour over the lamb chops. Marinate in the refrigerator for 2 hours. Heat an outdoor grill to medium. Place the chops on the grill in a single layer; grill for 2 to 3 minutes per side. Arrange on a serving platter. Top with Minty Red Wine Sauce.

To make the Minty Red Wine Sauce, heat the butter in a small saucepan and sauté the shallots until softened. Mix 1/4 cup red wine or broth with 1 teaspoon of cornstarch until smooth. Add to shallots, and then add allspice, currant jelly, mint, and remaining red wine or broth. Whisk on low heat for 2 minutes until sauce has thickened slightly. Strain and pour sauce over the grilled chops.

NOTE: Chops can be eaten informally by using the bone as a handle.

Lamb Riblets with Minty Red Wine Sauce

Indian Lamb Stew on Basmati Rice

1/4 cup vegetable oil

8 large cloves garlic, thinly sliced

2 tablespoons grated fresh ginger

1 teaspoon ground cinnamon

1/2 teaspoon ground cloves

1 tablespoon ground cumin

1 tablespoon ground coriander seeds

1/4 teaspoon cayenne pepper

1 bay leaf

1 tablespoon garam masala (optional)

3 pounds lamb stew meat or lamb shoulder, trimmed and cut into 1-inch pieces

3 onions, finely chopped

1 can (15 ounces) chopped tomatoes, drained

1 cup plain yogurt

1 cup water

1 teaspoon kosher salt

2 cups frozen peas, thawed

2 cups basmati rice cooked in 4 cups water

1/4 cup toasted pine nuts

Juice of 1 lemon

MAKES 6 TO 8 SERVINGS

In a large ovenproof pan, heat oil. Sauté garlic and ginger for 3 to 4 minutes on low heat until fragrant. Add cinnamon, cloves, cumin, coriander, cayenne pepper, bay leaf, and garam masala if using. Cook 1 minute more. Add lamb and onions, stirring often. Cook until lamb and onions are golden, over medium heat, for 8 to 10 minutes. Add tomatoes, yogurt, water, and salt. Cover and bake in a preheated oven at 350 degrees F for 1 hour. Add peas and lemon juice to lamb; pour into serving bowl over cooked basmati rice; sprinkle with pine nuts and serve at once.

Braised Beef Short Ribs with Wide Egg Noodles

Braised Beef Short Ribs with Wide Egg Noodles

SHORT RIBS

2   tablespoons olive oil
2   tablespoons butter
3 to 4 pounds boneless beef short ribs
1   tablespoon kosher salt
1   teaspoon ground black pepper
1   tablespoon Worcestershire sauce
½   cup bottled barbeque sauce
1   large onion, thinly sliced
2   carrots, peeled and thinly sliced on
     diagonal
2   cups beef broth

NOODLES

8   ounces wide egg noodles, cooked *al
     dente*
4   tablespoons butter
1   teaspoon kosher salt
½   cup finely chopped parsley

MAKES 4 TO 6 SERVINGS

In a large skillet with a lid, heat oil and butter. Add ribs; sprinkle on salt and pepper. Brown on one side over medium-high heat; turn, and sprinkle on more salt and pepper. Brown the other side. Add Worcestershire sauce, barbeque sauce, onion, carrots, and broth. Cover and simmer over low heat for 2 to 3 hours until beef ribs are tender. Heat the cooked egg noodles in butter to which salt and parsley have been added; toss just to heat through. Serve with Short Ribs.

Morrocan-Spiced Lamb Meatballs with Cucumber-Mint Sauce

LAMB MEATBALLS

2 pounds ground lamb
1 teaspoon curry powder
1 teaspoon cumin seeds
1 teaspoon turmeric
1 teaspoon fennel seeds
2 tablespoons olive oil
2 cloves garlic, minced
1 teaspoon kosher salt
1/8 teaspoon cayenne pepper

CUCUMBER-MINT SAUCE

1 English cucumber, finely chopped
1 small onion (about 1/2 cup), finely chopped
1/2 cup chopped fresh mint leaves
1 cup plain yogurt
1 tablespoon sugar
1 teaspoon kosher salt
1/4 teaspoon ground white pepper

MAKES ABOUT 24 MEATBALLS

In a medium bowl, combine the ground lamb, curry powder, cumin, turmeric, fennel, oil, garlic, salt, and cayenne pepper. Mix well and form into 1-inch meatballs. Place on a baking sheet and bake in a preheated oven at 375 degrees F for 15 minutes until browned and cooked through. Remove from oven and serve on platter with toothpicks and Cucumber-Mint Sauce on the side for dipping.

Combine all the ingredients for Cucumber-Mint Sauce in a medium bowl. Stir well. If you have a food processor, place ingredients in work bowl and pulse on and off 2 or 3 times to chop ingredients, not puree.

Pork Tenderloin Sandwiches with Onion Relish

2   pork tenderloins (about 1 pound
       each)
Zest and juice of 2 lemons
2   large sweet onions (such as Maui,
       Walla Walla, Mayan, or Vidalia),
       thinly sliced
2   cloves garlic, minced
¼   cup balsamic vinegar
1   tablespoon dried Italian seasoning
1   tablespoon yellow mustard seed or
       1 tablespoon coarse ground
       mustard
¼   cup extra virgin olive oil
1   teaspoon kosher salt
1   teaspoon coarse ground black
       pepper
2   dozen small buns (about 2 inches in
       diameter), sliced horizontally

MAKES ABOUT 24 SANDWICHES

Place the pork tenderloins in a shallow pan. In a small bowl, combine the lemon zest and juice, onions, garlic, balsamic vinegar, Italian seasoning, mustard seed or mustard, oil, salt, and pepper. Pour over the pork and marinate in refrigerator at least 1 hour and up to 4 hours. Remove pork from marinade, reserving the marinade for later use. Place tenderloins in a roasting pan and roast at 350 degrees F for 45 minutes.

While the pork is roasting, make the onion relish by pouring the reserved marinade in a saucepan and cooking over low heat for 15 to 20 minutes until the onions are soft.

When pork is done, cool to room temperature and thinly slice on diagonal. Arrange pork in a concentric circle on a serving platter, top with onion relish, and serve with buns.

NOTE: This is a perfect dish for a buffet or light luncheon.

Lemon Herb Roasted Chicken Legs and Thighs

8   chicken legs
8   chicken thighs
4   tablespoons butter, softened
3   cloves garlic, minced
2   tablespoons Italian seasoning or
     herbs de Provence
Zest and juice of 1 lemon
1   teaspoon salt
½   teaspoon ground black pepper
2   lemons, thinly sliced
1   cup chicken broth
4   Roma tomatoes, chopped
½   cup balsamic vinegar
Creamy Polenta (see page 182)

MAKES 4 TO 6 SERVINGS

Place the chicken pieces in a roasting pan. In a medium bowl, combine the butter, garlic, Italian seasoning or herbs, lemon zest and juice, salt, and pepper to make herb butter. Spread the butter mixture over the top of each piece of chicken. Place lemon slices on each piece. Place roasting pan in oven and bake at 350 degrees F for 30 minutes. Add broth to the pan after 15 minutes of roasting.

Remove the chicken from pan and pour pan drippings into a saucepan. Add tomatoes and balsamic vinegar. Cook over medium heat until reduced by half, about 5 minutes. Taste for seasoning. Pour sauce over chicken and serve with Creamy Polenta.

Lemon Herb Roasted Chicken Legs and Thighs

Italian Sausages with White Beans on Swiss Chard

SAUSAGE

2   tablespoons olive oil
4 to 5 sweet or hot Italian sausage links

BEANS

2   tablespoons olive oil
1   medium onion, thinly sliced
2   cloves garlic, minced
2   cans (15 ounces each) white northern beans or cannellini beans, drained
4   Roma tomatoes, diced small
¼   cup julienne-cut basil leaves
1   teaspoon kosher salt
¼   teaspoon ground black pepper

SWISS CHARD

3   tablespoons olive oil
2   bunches Swiss chard (red, green, or rainbow)
1   cup chicken broth
½   teaspoon red pepper flakes
1   teaspoon kosher salt
¼   cup grated Romano cheese

MAKES 4 SERVINGS

In a large skillet, heat olive oil and add sausage links. Cook over medium heat, covered, for 5 minutes; turn once and cook an additional 5 minutes. Remove the sausages from the pan and add 2 tablespoons of olive oil and onion. Sauté for 1 minute, then add garlic, beans, tomatoes, basil, salt, and pepper. Simmer on low for 2 to 3 minutes. Add the sausage links back in and cook another 10 minutes, until cooked through.

In a separate skillet, heat 3 tablespoons olive oil for the Swiss chard. Remove the tough ends of the chard, wash, and coarsely chop. Add chard, broth, red pepper flakes, and salt. Cover and steam for 3 to 5 minutes, stirring often, just until wilted. Place chard on a large serving platter and top with beans and sausages. Sprinkle grated Romano cheese on top.

Chicken and Black Bean Tostadas

1   can (15 ounces) black beans, drained and rinsed
1   pound cooked chicken breasts, cut into thin strips
2   Roma tomatoes, diced
¼   cup chopped fresh cilantro
1   teaspoon ground cumin
½   teaspoon dried ancho chili powder
Juice of 1 lime
2   green onions, thinly sliced
¼   cup vegetable oil
8   (6-inch) corn tortillas
Pico de Gallo (see page 98)
Classic Guacamole (see page 100)
1   cup crumbled queso fresco or seco (Mexican cheese)

MAKES 8 TOSTADAS

In a bowl, combine the black beans, cooked chicken, tomatoes, cilantro, cumin, ancho chili powder, lime juice, and green onions.

Heat 1 tablespoon vegetable oil in a 10-inch skillet. Add corn tortillas, one at a time, and cook for 30 seconds per side. Add 1 tablespoon oil to skillet before cooking each tortilla. Place cooked tortillas on paper towels to drain. While still hot, top the tortillas with the chicken mixture, Pico de Gallo, and Classic Guacamole. Add crumbled cheese on top. Serve at once.

Maple Pecan Pork Tenderloin

2   pork tenderloins, about 1 pound each
1   large sweet onion (such as Maui, Mayan, Walla Walla, or Vidalia), peeled and thinly sliced into 1/2-inch rings
2   tablespoons olive oil
³/₄ cup pure maple syrup
¹/₂ cup honey
1   cup chopped pecans
1   tablespoon Dijon mustard or 1 tablespoon mustard seeds, black or white
1   tablespoon chili powder
1   tablespoon dried thyme leaves
1   tablespoon kosher salt
¹/₂ teaspoon dried red pepper flakes

MAKES 6 TO 8 SERVINGS

Place pork tenderloins on a work surface; cut each in half, crosswise. Place the 4 pieces in a ceramic or glass shallow pan. Top with the onion, distributing evenly over the pork. In a separate bowl, combine the oil, maple syrup, honey, pecans, mustard, chili powder, thyme, salt, and red pepper flakes. Pour over pork; cover with plastic and refrigerate for at least 2 hours and up to 8 hours.

Heat an outdoor grill to medium. Remove pork from marinade and reserve marinade for later use. Place the pork on the grill along with the sliced onion from the marinade. Turn pork after 10 minutes. When the onion is cooked and golden, remove from the grill to keep from burning. After 20 minutes, test pork for doneness; meat thermometer should read 140 degrees F to 145 degrees F in center. Allow pork to rest for 5 minutes before slicing.

While pork is still on the grill, heat the reserved marinade in a small saucepan for 8 to 10 minutes until thickened. Taste for seasoning. Thinly slice pork and serve with grilled onion and drizzled marinade on top.

NOTE: This is an easy and elegant summertime entrée; serve with coleslaw such as Easy Summer Slaw (see page 114), Parslied Potatoes and Parsnips Parmesan (see page 184), or on bed of spinach or arugula leaves. Try it in sandwiches, served in dollar or potato rolls.

Pasta and Grains

THE RECIPES

Asparagus, Peas, and Chive Risotto

ASPARAGUS

2   tablespoons olive oil
1   bunch fresh asparagus spears, ends trimmed, cut into 1-inch pieces
1   teaspoon kosher salt

RISOTTO

6   tablespoons butter, divided
2   large shallots, chopped
2   cups Arborio rice (small grain Italian rice)
½   teaspoon kosher salt
¼   teaspoon ground black pepper
6   cups warmed chicken broth
2   cups petite green peas, thawed if frozen
1   cup grated Parmesan cheese
½   cup chopped fresh chives (for garnish)
¼   cup grated Parmesan cheese (for garnish)

MAKES 4 TO 6 SERVINGS

In a medium skillet, heat olive oil and add asparagus and salt. Toss; cook over medium heat for 3 to 4 minutes, stirring often, until bright green. Set aside.

In a large saucepan, heat 4 tablespoons butter and sauté shallots until soft, about 4 minutes. Add rice, stirring to coat with butter and shallots. Add salt, pepper, and 1 cup of broth. Stir; cook over low heat for 4 to 5 minutes, stirring often, until liquid is absorbed. Add another cup of broth (continuing the process so that the liquid is being absorbed by the rice); repeat until all the broth is used, adding just a cup at a time, stirring rice often. After 25 minutes or so, rice should be tender. Add peas, cooked asparagus, cheese, and remaining 2 tablespoons of butter. Cook 1 minute more over low heat. Remove from heat. Serve risotto with chopped fresh chives and grated cheese as garnish.

Asparagus, Peas, and Chive Risotto

Autumn Orecchiette with Cauliflower

1	pound orecchiette ("little ears") pasta
2	tablespoons extra virgin olive oil
2	tablespoons butter
3	cloves garlic, minced
¼	cup pine nuts
1	medium head cauliflower, cut into 1-inch florets
2	cups peeled and diced butternut squash
1	red bell pepper, cored and cut into ½-inch dice
3	cups chicken or vegetable broth, divided
½	cup white wine
½	cup golden raisins
1	teaspoon kosher salt
¼	teaspoon ground black pepper
1	cup grated Romano or Parmesan cheese
½	cup chopped fresh Italian parsley

MAKES 4 SERVINGS

Cook pasta *al dente*, drain, and set aside. In a large skillet, heat oil and butter and add garlic and pine nuts. Sauté for 30 seconds, and then add cauliflower, squash, and red bell pepper. Sauté for 2 to 3 minutes; add 2 cups broth, wine, raisins, salt, and pepper. Cover and simmer for 5 to 8 minutes until squash is tender. Add remaining 1 cup of broth and reserved pasta; toss and cook until pasta is heated through, about 2 minutes. Pour into a large serving bowl, add grated cheese and parsley, and toss to combine. Serve at once.

NOTE: This makes a colorful autumn dish, with hues of gold and red, and a touch of sweetness from the raisins. If orecchiette is not available, substitute any other small 1-inch shaped pasta, such as shells, farfalle, penne, or rigatoni.

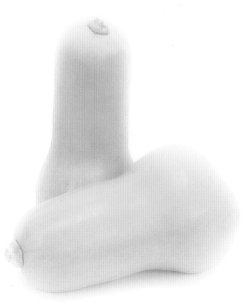

Farfalle with Creamy Peas and Prosciutto

1 pound imported farfalle (bow tie) pasta
2 tablespoons butter
2 tablespoons olive oil
2 shallots, chopped
2 cloves garlic, minced
¼ pound prosciutto, diced
1 package (16 ounces) frozen petite peas, thawed
1 cup chicken broth
1½ cups heavy cream
1 teaspoon kosher salt
¼ teaspoon ground white pepper
2 cups grated Romano cheese, divided

MAKES 4 TO 6 SERVINGS

Cook pasta *al dente*, drain, and set aside. In a large saucepan, heat butter and oil and sauté shallots for 2 minutes over low heat. Add garlic and prosciutto and sauté for 3 to 4 minutes. Stir in peas, broth, cream, salt, and pepper. Cook for another 3 minutes until sauce slightly thickens. Stir the reserved pasta and 1 cup cheese into sauce, tossing for about 30 seconds. Serve at once topped with remaining cheese for garnish.

Fettuccine with Butternut Squash and Porcini Mushrooms

1 pound imported fettuccine pasta
4 cups peeled and diced butternut squash
½ teaspoon ground cinnamon
2 tablespoons extra virgin olive oil
4 tablespoons butter
¼ cup dried porcini mushrooms, rehydrated in 2 cups hot water
2 cloves garlic, minced
½ cup chopped fresh sage leaves
8 ounces mascarpone cheese
1 cup chicken or beef broth
½ cup grated Romano or Parmesan cheese

MAKES 4 SERVINGS

Cook pasta *al dente,* drain, and set aside. In a medium bowl, toss the squash, cinnamon, and oil. Place the squash in a single layer on a baking sheet and roast in at 375 degrees F for 20 minutes, tossing once during cooking process.

While squash is roasting, heat butter in a large skillet. Squeeze the liquid from the mushrooms and reserve. Sauté garlic and mushrooms in the butter for 5 minutes. Add sage, mascarpone cheese, reserved mushroom liquid, and broth. Cook another 2 to 3 minutes on low heat; stir in the roasted squash and cooked fettuccine. Cook for 1 minute more, until pasta is heated through. Sprinkle with cheese, toss, and serve at once.

BLT Farfalle

BLT Farfalle

1 pound imported farfalle (bow tie) pasta
2 tablespoons olive oil
¼ pound pancetta (Italian cured bacon), cut into small dice*
1 large shallot, peeled and chopped
2 large cloves garlic, minced
6 to 8 Roma tomatoes, chopped
1 teaspoon kosher salt
¼ teaspoon coarse ground black pepper
1 cup white wine, chicken broth, or vegetable broth
1 cup shaved Parmesan or Romano cheese**
5 to 6 cups arugula leaves or baby spinach leaves

MAKES 4 TO 6 SERVINGS

Cook pasta *al dente*, drain, and set aside in a large bowl. In a large skillet, heat oil. Add pancetta and cook for 4 to 5 minutes over low heat until crispy. Add shallot and garlic; cook 1 minute more. Add tomatoes, salt, pepper, and wine or broth; simmer on low heat for 5 minutes. Stir the cooked pasta into the tomato sauce, just to heat through. Pour into a large serving bowl and add the cheese and arugula or spinach. Toss to mix thoroughly. Serve at once.

*If not available, any good quality bacon will do.

**You can use a vegetable peeler to make shavings from a wedge of cheese.

Pesto alla Trapani and Sausage Pasta

PESTO

1   cup fresh Italian parsley
½   cup basil leaves
½   cup sliced almonds
2   Roma tomatoes, coarsely chopped
2   large cloves garlic, coarsely chopped
1   teaspoon salt
½   cup grated Romano cheese
½   to 1 cup extra virgin olive oil

SAUSAGE MIXTURE

2   tablespoons extra virgin olive oil
½   pound mild Italian sausage in bulk
½   cup chopped onion

PASTA

1   pound imported tubular-shaped pasta (such as penne, rigatoni, or ziti), cooked *al dente* and drained
1   cup grated Romano or Parmesan cheese

MAKES 4 TO 6 SERVINGS

To make the pesto, place all ingredients except oil in work bowl of food processor. Puree until all ingredients are well combined. Slowly add the olive oil while motor is running to form a smooth pesto. Taste for seasoning.

In a large skillet, heat 2 tablespoons oil and cook sausage and onion until sausage is cooked through, crumbling as you cook. Remove from heat, add pesto and cooked pasta, tossing well. Return to heat and cook for 1 minute more on low heat. Transfer to a large serving platter, top with cheese, and serve at once.

NOTE: This is a variation of a dish I so fondly remember dining on in Trapani, Sicily. Its bold, rich flavors make for a wonderful one-dish meal.

Rigatoni with Sausage and Bechamel Spinach

1   pound imported rigatoni pasta,
     cooked a little under *al dente* and
     drained
1   pound Italian sausage in bulk
12   cups fresh spinach leaves, blanched
     in water and drained
6   tablespoons butter
2   shallots, peeled and diced
6   tablespoons flour
2   cups milk
1   cup chicken broth
½   teaspoon nutmeg
2   cups grated Parmesan cheese
½   teaspoon white pepper
½   teaspoon kosher salt

MAKES 6 TO 8 SERVINGS

Place undercooked and drained rigatoni in a large mixing bowl. In a medium skillet, cook sausage, crumbling as you cook; drain off excess fat. Place in bowl with pasta. In the same skillet, cook spinach with a little water and salt for 2 to 3 minutes until wilted. Drain and squeeze excess liquid from spinach. Place the spinach in the bowl with pasta and sausage.

In a medium saucepan, heat butter. Sauté shallots until soft. Add flour; cook over low heat for 2 minutes, stirring often. Slowly whisk in the milk, broth, and nutmeg. Whisk over medium heat until sauce has thickened, about 5 minutes. Add cheese, pepper, and salt. Pour into bowl with pasta and sausage. Toss well. Pour entire mixture into a 4-quart baking dish or into individual au gratin dishes. Cover with foil and bake at 350 degrees F for 30 minutes if using large baking dish, or 15 minutes if using individual dishes. Remove foil and bake an additional 5 minutes to brown the top lightly.

Free-Form Ravioli with Crabmeat and Shrimp

4 tablespoons butter
2 large shallots, peeled and chopped
1 medium zucchini, thinly sliced or julienned
2 carrots, peeled, thinly sliced or julienned
1 cup heavy cream
2 cups chicken broth
3 tablespoons tomato paste
1 teaspoon kosher salt
½ teaspoon ground white pepper
½ pound crabmeat or lobster meat
½ pound raw shrimp, peeled and coarsely chopped
¾ cup chopped fresh chives, divided
½ cup chopped fresh basil leaves
2 quarts water
1 teaspoon kosher salt
12 large wonton wrappers (about 5 x 5 inches)

MAKES 6 SERVINGS

In a medium saucepan, heat butter. Add shallots, zucchini, and carrots. Sauté for 2 to 3 minutes, then add cream, broth, tomato paste, salt, and pepper. Simmer for 3 minutes until thickened slightly. Add crabmeat or lobster meat and shrimp to saucepan. Cook for 2 minutes until shrimp are pink, but be careful not to boil. Add 1/4 cup chives and basil to sauce.

While making the sauce, bring 2 quarts of water with salt to a boil. Add wonton wrappers, two at a time, and cook for 1 minute. Remove the wrappers from the water with a slotted spoon and place on a platter lined with paper towels. When all are cooked, place two wrappers in each of six serving bowls and ladle in some of the crabmeat-shrimp sauce over the free-form "ravioli." Sprinkle with remaining chives and serve at once.

Free-Form Ravioli with Crabmeat and Shrimp

Pasta Con Ceci
(Pasta with Garbanzo Beans)

2   tablespoons olive oil
1   medium onion, chopped
2   ribs celery, sliced
2   carrots, peeled and sliced
2   cloves garlic, minced
⅛   teaspoon crushed red pepper flakes
1   can (14 ounces) chopped tomatoes
4   cups vegetable broth
2   cups water
1   can (15 ounces) garbanzo beans
     with liquid
1   cup dry ditalini pasta (or other small
     pasta such as shells, farfallini, or
     orzo)
1   teaspoon kosher salt
1   tablespoon chopped fresh rosemary
1   tablespoon chopped fresh basil
4 to 5 cups fresh spinach leaves
1   cup grated Romano or Parmesan
     cheese

In a medium saucepan, heat oil and sauté onion, celery, and carrots for 3 to 5 minutes over low heat, stirring often. Add garlic and red pepper flakes; sauté 1 minute more. Add tomatoes, broth, and water; cover and simmer for 10 minutes. Add beans, pasta, and salt. Cook, uncovered, for 10 minutes until pasta is cooked through. Stir in rosemary, basil, and spinach; cook on low heat until spinach is just wilted. Serve at once with cheese on top.

NOTE: This quick and easy, yet flavorful thick soup is perfect on a cold winter night. In less than 30 minutes a hearty dish can be on the table.

Penne Oi Quattro Formaggi (Pasta with Four Cheeses)

1	pound imported penne pasta
1	tablespoon olive oil
6	tablespoons butter
¾	cup flour
3	cups whole milk
1	cup shredded Parmesan or Romano cheese
1	cup blue cheese, gorgonzola, cambozola, or blue costello
1	cup diced Italian fontina or provolone cheese
1	cup diced mozzarella cheese
¼	teaspoon grated nutmeg
¼	teaspoon ground white pepper
1	teaspoon kosher salt
1	cup bread crumbs
¼	cup chopped fresh Italian parsley

MAKES 6 SERVINGS

Cook pasta a little under *al dente*, drain, and toss with olive oil; place in a large mixing bowl. In a medium saucepan, heat butter and stir in flour; mix until combined. Whisk in milk slowly, and then cook over low heat until thickened. Add all the cheeses, nutmeg, pepper, and salt. Stir over low heat until cheeses have melted, then pour over the pasta and mix to combine. Place pasta with cheese sauce in a greased 4-quart baking dish, and then sprinkle on the bread crumbs and Italian parsley. (Or you can use individual ramekins or au gratin dishes if you prefer.) The recipe can be made ahead up to this point, covered with plastic wrap, and refrigerated until ready to use. Bake, uncovered, for 20 minutes in a preheated oven at 375 degrees F until bubbly.

Paparadelle alla Primavera

Paparadelle alla Primavera

1   pound imported paparadelle or other wide flat pasta (such as tagliatelle or fettuccine)

2   tablespoons butter

2   tablespoons olive oil

½   red onion, thinly sliced

2   large cloves garlic, minced

1   bunch fresh asparagus, ends trimmed and cut into 2-inch pieces

1   red bell pepper, cored and thinly sliced

1   can (15 ounces) artichoke hearts, quartered and drained

2   cups chicken or vegetable broth

2   cups frozen peas, thawed

1   large carrot, peeled and thinly sliced or julienned

1½   cups half-and-half

1   teaspoon kosher salt

¼   teaspoon ground black pepper

¼   cup chopped fresh chives

1   cup grated Romano or Parmesan cheese

MAKES 4 TO 6 SERVINGS

Cook pasta *al dente*, drain, and set aside. In a large skillet, heat butter and oil. Sauté onion until softened; add garlic, asparagus, and bell pepper. Cook for 2 minutes. Add artichokes, broth, peas, carrot, half-and-half, salt, and pepper. Simmer for 2 to 3 minutes until sauce has thickened slightly. Stir the cooked pasta into sauce; toss until pasta has heated through. Transfer to serving bowl and top with chopped chives and cheese.

Tortellini with Rapini and Beans

¼ pound pancetta, chopped
2 tablespoons olive oil
1 small onion, diced
2 cloves garlic, minced
Pinch red pepper flakes
2 bunches rapini (broccoli rabe), ends trimmed and coarsely chopped
1 cup water
2 cans (15 ounces each) small white beans, drained
2 large tomatoes, chopped
1 pound cheese tortellini, cooked *al dente* and drained
2 cups vegetable or chicken broth
¼ cup grated Romano cheese

MAKES 6 TO 8 SERVINGS

In a large sauté pan, brown pancetta in oil. Add onion, garlic, red pepper flakes, rapini, and water. Cover and cook over medium heat for 2 to 3 minutes. Stir in the white beans and tomatoes, and cook for another 5 minutes. Taste for seasoning. Add the cooked tortellini and broth; stir until heated through, about 2 minutes. Serve with Romano cheese sprinkled on top.

NOTE: Rapini is Italian broccoli, which has a bitter, but delectably distinct flavor. If it is not available, substitute 2 bunches broccolini or 2 pounds broccoli florets.

Lemon Mint Rice

2 tablespoons butter
¼ cup chopped onion
1 cup long grain rice
2 cups vegetable or chicken stock
Zest of 1 lemon
⅛ teaspoon ground white pepper
½ teaspoon salt
½ cup chopped fresh mint leaves
¼ cup toasted sliced or slivered almonds

MAKES 4 SERVINGS

In a small saucepan, heat butter and sauté onion until softened. Add rice and sauté for 1 minute. Add stock, lemon zest, pepper, and salt. Cover and simmer for 20 minutes until rice is cooked through and liquid is absorbed. Stir in mint and almonds. Taste for seasoning.

Tortellini with Rapini and Beans

Frittata de Pasta

¼	pound imported pasta (linguine, spaghetti, or cappellini)
2	tablespoons butter
¼	cup sliced onion
1	zucchini, thinly sliced
2	Roma tomatoes, thinly sliced
8	large eggs
1½	cups half-and-half
¼	cup chopped fresh basil
¼	cup grated Romano cheese
1	teaspoon kosher salt
¼	teaspoon black pepper
2	tablespoons olive oil

MAKES 6 TO 8 SERVINGS

Cook pasta *al dente*, drain, and set aside. In a nonstick, ovenproof 10-inch pan, heat butter and sauté onion, zucchini, and tomatoes for 2 minutes. In a bowl, beat together eggs, half-and-half, basil, and cheese. Add sautéed vegetables, cooked pasta, salt, and pepper. Mix well. Heat oil in the 10-inch pan, add the egg mixture, and cook over medium heat for 3 minutes, then transfer to a preheated oven at 400 degrees F and bake for 15 to 20 minutes or until the eggs are set and puffed. Remove from oven, allow the frittata to set for a minute, then unmold onto serving platter and cut into 6 to 8 wedges.

Roasted Autumn Squash Risotto

2   pounds butternut or banana squash,
      peeled and cut into ½-inch pieces
¼   cup plus 2 tablespoons extra virgin
      olive oil, divided
1   teaspoon kosher salt
2   tablespoons butter
2   leeks, white part only, thinly sliced
2   cups Arborio rice
6   cups chicken or vegetable broth
½   cup dry white wine
½   cup half-and-half
¼   cup chopped fresh sage leaves
½   cup grated Parmesan cheese
1   teaspoon kosher salt
½   teaspoon ground black pepper
Sage leaves (for garnish)
Shaved Parmesan cheese (for garnish)

MAKES 4 TO 6 SERVINGS

Place the cut squash on a baking sheet, drizzle with 1/4 cup olive oil, and sprinkle with salt. Bake in a preheated oven at 375 degrees F for 30 minutes. Set aside.

In a medium saucepan, heat remaining oil and butter. Add leeks and sauté for 3 to 5 minutes, tossing often, until leeks are softened and lightly golden. Stir in the rice, toss again, and then add the broth, one cup at a time, stirring the rice until the liquid is completely absorbed. (This process of stirring and adding the broth will take about 25 minutes.) Stir in the cooked squash, wine, half-and-half, sage, cheese, salt, and pepper. Cook for another 5 minutes over low heat; taste for seasoning. Spoon into serving bowls. Garnish each serving with sage leaves and Parmesan cheese.

Sauces and Salsas

THE RECIPES

Pico de Gallo

Mango-Avocado Salsa

Corn-Tomato-Mint Salsa

Classic Guacamole

Grilled Peach and Red Pepper Salsa

Lemon Parsley Aioli

Spicy Ginger-Peanut Sauce

Pineapple Salsa

Creamy Cilantro and Jalapeño Sauce

Honey-Orange-Sesame Dipping Sauce

Greek Cucumber-Yogurt Sauce

Creamy Chipotle-Tomato Sauce

Pico de Gallo

8 large Roma tomatoes, coarsely chopped
1 jalapeño pepper, cored and chopped
½ red onion, coarsely chopped
1 cup fresh cilantro leaves
1 large clove garlic, chopped
1 teaspoon kosher salt
Juice of 1 lime
2 tablespoons olive oil

MAKES ABOUT 2 CUPS

Place all ingredients in food processor. Pulse on and off until salsa is chunky, not pureed, about 5 to 6 pulses. Taste for seasoning.

Mango-Avocado Salsa

1 large mango, peeled and diced
2 large avocados, peeled and diced
¼ cup chopped fresh cilantro
¼ cup chopped red onion
1 jalapeño pepper, cored and diced
Juice of 2 limes
2 tablespoons canola oil
½ teaspoon kosher salt
1 teaspoon sugar
Cilantro leaves (for garnish)
Lime slices (for garnish)

MAKES ABOUT 2 CUPS

In a medium bowl, combine all ingredients except cilantro leaves and lime slices. Toss gently. Garnish with cilantro leaves and lime slices.

Corn-Tomato-Mint Salsa

1 package (16 ounces) frozen white or yellow corn kernels, thawed
2 large tomatoes, coarsely chopped
½ cup chopped fresh mint leaves
2 cloves garlic, minced
1 teaspoon kosher salt
Pinch red pepper flakes
2 tablespoons white wine or cider vinegar
¼ cup canola oil

MAKES ABOUT 3 CUPS

Combine all ingredients in a bowl and mix well. This recipe can be made several hours ahead and kept refrigerated.

NOTE: I like to serve the Seared Salmon and Leek-Carrot Sauce (see page 140) on a bed of this salsa.

Pico de Gallo

Classic Guacamole

4	large ripe avocados

Juice of 2 limes
1	large clove garlic, minced
1/4	cup finely chopped red onion
2	Roma tomatoes, finely chopped
1/4	cup finely chopped cilantro
1/2	teaspoon kosher salt
1	jalapeño pepper, cored and diced

MAKES ABOUT 3 CUPS

Peel the avocados, remove pit, and chop. Place in a medium bowl and toss with lime juice. With a fork or potato masher, mash avocado. Stir in the garlic, red onion, tomatoes, cilantro, salt, and jalapeño. Taste for seasoning; add more salt if needed.

Grilled Peach and Red Pepper Salsa

2	firm peaches
2	tablespoons olive oil, divided
2	tablespoons chopped fresh mint
2	tablespoons chopped fresh basil
1	large clove garlic, minced
1/4	cup chopped red onion
1	large red bell pepper, cored and finely chopped
2	tablespoons cider vinegar
1	teaspoon kosher salt

MAKES ABOUT 2 CUPS

Pit peaches, cut them in half, and brush with 1 tablespoon oil. Heat an outdoor grill or grill pan. Place oiled peaches on grill, cut side down, and grill for 3 to 4 minutes. Remove from grill and cool slightly. Remove peel and discard; dice peaches. In a medium bowl, combine the diced peaches, remaining oil, mint, basil, garlic, onion, red bell pepper, vinegar, and salt. Toss gently. Refrigerate until ready to serve.

Lemon Parsley Aioli

1	cup Italian parsley leaves

Zest and juice of 2 lemons
2	cloves garlic
1	teaspoon kosher salt
1/4	teaspoon ground black pepper
1/2	cup mayonnaise
1/4	cup olive oil

MAKES ABOUT 1 CUP

Place parsley, lemon zest and juice, garlic, salt, pepper, and mayonnaise in a blender. Puree until smooth. Slowly pour in the oil while the motor is running until aioli is thickened. Taste for seasoning.

NOTE: Use this as a dip for skewered chicken or seafood; drizzle over grilled meats, poultry, or seafood; or use as a dipping sauce for artichoke leaves.

Spicy Ginger-Peanut Sauce

2 tablespoons peanut or canola oil
2 cloves garlic, minced
1 tablespoon minced ginger
1 teaspoon Asian hot chili garlic sauce*
1/2 cup soy sauce
3 tablespoons hoisin sauce
1 tablespoon sesame oil
2 tablespoons sugar
3/4 cup creamy peanut butter
1 1/2 cups chicken broth

MAKES ABOUT 2 CUPS

In a medium skillet or wok, heat oil over medium heat until smoky, about 2 minutes, then add garlic and ginger; stir-fry for 2 minutes, add hot chili garlic sauce, soy sauce, hoisin sauce, sesame oil, sugar, peanut butter, and broth. Whisk over medium heat for another 2 to 3 minutes until all ingredients are combined. Remove from heat. Cool to room temperature or chill until ready to serve.

NOTE: Use this as a dipping sauce for chicken skewers or grilled shrimp, or toss into a noodle salad with steamed vegetables.

*Use more if you like your sauce hotter.

Pineapple Salsa

2 cups finely chopped fresh pineapple
1 red bell pepper, cored and finely chopped
1 cup jicama, peeled and chopped
1 jalapeño pepper, cored and chopped
1/4 cup chopped red onion
2 tablespoons cider vinegar
1/4 cup vegetable or peanut oil
1/2 cup chopped fresh cilantro
1 teaspoon kosher salt
1 teaspoon sugar

MAKES ABOUT 3 CUPS

Combine all ingredients in a bowl and serve.

NOTE: This recipe works well as a salsa for tostadas, as a dip for chips and vegetables, or over grilled meats and seafood.

Creamy Cilantro and Jalapeño Sauce

1   cup Ranch dressing
1   cup fresh cilantro leaves
1   jalapeño pepper, cored and
     coarsely chopped
Juice and zest of 2 limes
1   teaspoon chili powder
1   clove garlic, coarsely chopped

MAKES ABOUT 1 1/2 CUPS

Place all the ingredients in a food processor or blender, and blend until smooth. Taste for seasoning. Sauce should be smooth and creamy. Refrigerate until ready to serve.

NOTE: Use as a topping for beef and bean tostadas or as a dressing on any green salad.

Honey-Orange-Sesame Dipping Sauce

¼   cup honey
¼   cup rice wine vinegar
¼   cup soy sauce
2   teaspoons grated fresh ginger root
2   teaspoons Asian hot garlic chili
     sauce
1   teaspoon sesame oil
Zest of 1 large orange
¼   cup chopped fresh cilantro
¼   cup chopped fresh mint leaves
2   tablespoons toasted sesame seeds

MAKES 1 CUP

In a bowl, whisk together all ingredients. Cover and chill until ready to serve.

NOTE: Serve with wontons, grilled salmon skewers, or grilled chicken skewers.

Greek Cucumber-Yogurt Sauce

1   cup plain yogurt
1   clove garlic, minced
2   tablespoons minced onion
¼   cup chopped fresh mint leaves
2   tablespoons chopped fresh dill
1   teaspoon sugar
½   teaspoon kosher salt
1   medium cucumber, peeled, seeded,
     and finely diced

MAKES ABOUT 1 1/2 CUPS

In a bowl, combine all ingredients; stir, taste for seasoning, and refrigerate until ready to serve.

NOTE: Greek Cucumber-Yogurt Sauce is great served with Lamb Riblets (page 62), Moroccan-Spiced Lamb Meatballs (page 68), or warmed pita bread.

Creamy Chipotle-Tomato Sauce

1   pepper from 7-ounce can of chipotle
     peppers in adobo sauce, coarsely
     chopped
2   Roma tomatoes, coarsely chopped
1   clove garlic, coarsely chopped
2   green onions, ends trimmed, cut into
     1-inch pieces
1   cup mayonnaise
1   cup sour cream
¼   cup half-and-half

MAKES ABOUT 2 CUPS

In a food processor or blender, combine all ingredients and process until smooth. Taste for seasoning. Refrigerate until ready to serve.

NOTE: Use as a dipping sauce for chips and crudites, as a topping for beef and bean tostadas, or tossed into a green salad as a dressing.

Salads

THE RECIPES

Garden Herb Chicken Salad

CHICKEN SALAD

1½ to 2 pounds grilled boneless and
 skinless chicken breasts, cut into
 1-inch dice
2 tablespoons fresh French tarragon
2 tablespoons fresh mint
2 tablespoons fresh rosemary
2 tablespoons fresh oregano
2 tablespoons fresh chives
1 red bell pepper, cored and thinly
 sliced
2 cucumbers, peeled, seeded, and
 thinly sliced
2 oranges, peeled and thinly sliced
1 red onion, thinly sliced
½ cup toasted cashews, almonds, or
 pecans
4 to 6 cups baby spinach leaves
Whole chives (for garnish)
Fresh mint leaves (for garnish)
Orange slices (for garnish)

DRESSING

¼ cup sherry vinegar
1 tablespoon Dijon mustard
1 teaspoon kosher salt
2 shallots, finely diced
¼ teaspoon black pepper
½ cup olive oil

MAKES 4 SERVINGS

Place chicken, herbs, bell pepper, cucumbers, oranges, onion, and nuts in a large bowl. Line a serving platter with the baby spinach leaves. In a small bowl, whisk together the ingredients for the dressing. This can be made a day or two ahead. Toss the dressing in the chicken mixture at the last minute and serve on baby spinach. Garnish with chives, mint leaves, and/or orange slices.

In a mixing bowl, whisk together all the dressing ingredients. This can be made a day or two ahead.

NOTE: This is the perfect summer dish to prepare on the patio, take along on picnics, or serve as a light lunch.

Garden Herb Chicken Salad

Asian Scallop Salad

SCALLOPS

1   pound large sea scallops (about 12 to 16 per pound)
1   teaspoon kosher salt
1   teaspoon Chinese Five Spice
½   teaspoon hot chili oil
2   tablespoons canola or vegetable oil

SALAD

½   cup fresh mint leaves
1   cup fresh cilantro leaves
1   cup matchstick carrots
½   red onion, thinly sliced
2   green onions, thinly sliced on diagonal
4   cups baby spinach leaves
1   small head Nappa cabbage, cored and thinly sliced
    Fresh mint sprigs (for garnish)

DRESSING

½   cup soy sauce
¼   cup rice wine vinegar
2   tablespoons canola or vegetable oil
2   tablespoons hoisin sauce
1   tablespoon sesame oil
1   tablespoon brown sugar
¼   teaspoon hot chili oil
2   cloves garlic, minced
¼   cup toasted sesame seeds

MAKES 4 SERVINGS

Pat the scallops dry with paper towels. In a bowl, combine the salt, Chinese Five Spice, hot chili oil, and canola or vegetable oil. Rub the mixture on both sides of scallops. Heat a large skillet or grill pan and sear the scallops for 3 to 4 minutes per side over medium-high heat. Set aside.

In a large mixing bowl, toss together all ingredients for salad except mint sprigs. Place on 4 individual plates. In a separate bowl, mix together all ingredients for dressing, whisking well.

To serve, top each salad plate with 3 to 4 scallops, drizzle on some of the dressing, and garnish with mint sprigs.

Cajun Shrimp and Andouille Salad

SHRIMP MARINADE

1	pound raw jumbo shrimp, peeled and deveined
1	clove garlic, minced
2	tablespoons olive oil
1	tablespoon spicy Cajun seasoning
1/2	pound spicy andouille sausage, cut into 1-inch pieces

SALAD

4	cups baby spinach leaves
1	red bell pepper, cored and thinly sliced
1/2	red onion, thinly sliced
1	pomegranate, seeded (optional)
1	cup blue cheese, crumbled*
1	cup toasted chopped walnuts

DRESSING

1/4	cup red wine vinegar
	Juice and zest of 1 orange
1	teaspoon kosher salt
1/2	teaspoon ground black pepper
1	tablespoon Dijon or other spicy mustard
1/2	cup extra virgin olive oil

MAKES 4 SERVINGS

In a medium bowl, combine the shrimp, garlic, oil, and Cajun seasoning. Marinate several hours, if time allows. Heat a medium skillet over high heat for 1 minute, add shrimp and toss until pink, about 2 minutes. Transfer shrimp to a bowl. Add andouille sausage to the skillet and cook over medium heat until cooked through, about 5 to 8 minutes, tossing often. Add cooked sausage to shrimp.

In a medium bowl, toss all ingredients for salad. In a small bowl, whisk all ingredients for dressing. The dressing can be made a day ahead.

Place the salad on a decorative platter; top with shrimp and sausage mixture. Drizzle on the dressing just before serving.

*I prefer Maytag blue cheese in this salad.

Fennel, Orange, and Pecan Salad

SALAD

1 tablespoon butter

1 large red onion, thinly sliced

1 large bulb fennel, outer layer and fronds removed, thinly sliced

2 large oranges (navel, Cara Cara, or Valencia), peeled and thinly sliced

½ cup toasted pecans

½ cup crumbled feta, blue, or goat cheese

6 to 8 cups mixed spring greens

DRESSING

2 tablespoons balsamic vinegar

2 tablespoons red wine vinegar

1 tablespoon Dijon mustard

1 tablespoon mayonnaise or sour cream

¼ cup chopped fresh chives or 2 green onions, thinly sliced

1 teaspoon kosher salt

1 teaspoon sugar

¼ teaspoon ground black pepper

½ cup extra virgin olive oil

MAKES 4 SERVINGS

In a medium skillet, heat butter. Sauté onion in butter for 10 minutes over low heat. Cool. Place fennel, orange slices, pecans, cheese, and sautéed onions in a large salad bowl. Toss gently. Add mixed greens and toss again.

In a small bowl, whisk together all ingredients for dressing until emulsified. This can be done a day ahead. Just before serving, drizzle just enough dressing over the salad to coat lightly.

Fennel, Orange, and Pecan Salad

Arugula and Asparagus Pasta Salad

SALAD

1 pound imported Italian pasta (such as penne, ziti, gemelli, or rotini)
1 tablespoon olive oil
4 to 6 cups arugula leaves, coarsely chopped
1 bunch fresh asparagus, ends trimmed, cut into 1-inch pieces, blanched and drained
1 package (16 ounces) frozen peas, thawed
1 cup pitted kalamata olives, coarsely chopped
½ cup shaved Parmesan cheese*

DRESSING

½ cup extra virgin olive oil
2 cloves garlic, minced
¼ teaspoon red pepper flakes
Zest and juice of 1 lemon
1 teaspoon kosher salt
½ teaspoon ground black pepper

MAKES 6 TO 8 SERVINGS

Cook pasta to *al dente*, drain, and rinse. Place cooked pasta in a bowl with the oil to prevent it from sticking. Toss well. Add the arugula, asparagus, peas, and olives.

In a small bowl, combine the ingredients for dressing. Stir into salad just before serving. Top with Parmesan cheese.

*Use a vegetable peeler to "shave" wedges of cheese into thin strips.

Grilled Calamari Salad with Mango

CALAMARI

1	pound calamari rings and tentacles
2	tablespoons soy sauce
2	cloves garlic, minced
1	serrano chili, finely diced
2	tablespoons olive oil

SALAD

4	cups baby spinach
1	red onion, thinly sliced
1	mango, peeled and diced
1	cup cilantro leaves, chopped
2	cups jicama (approximately), peeled and cut into thin strips

DRESSING

2	tablespoons red wine vinegar
½	cup olive oil
1	teaspoon kosher salt
½	teaspoon black pepper

MAKES 4 SERVINGS

Combine the calamari, soy sauce, garlic, serrano chili, and oil in a bowl; marinate for 1 hour. Heat a grill pan or an outdoor grill over medium heat; use a barbeque basket so the calamari do not fall into the grill. Drain the calamari from the marinade, then quickly stir-fry in grill pan or basket on the grill for 1 to 2 minutes, tossing often. The rings should be opaque and the tentacles should be purple. Place in large serving bowl.

Combine salad ingredients in bowl with the grilled calamari. In a separate bowl, whisk together the dressing ingredients and then toss into salad.

Easy Summer Slaw

SALAD

2   packages (16 ounces each) prepared coleslaw*

1   red bell pepper, cored and diced

½   red onion, finely chopped

½   cup chopped fresh chives

2   Granny Smith apples, cored and julienned or shredded

DRESSING

1   cup mayonnaise

½   cup canola oil

¼   cup red wine vinegar

1   tablespoon poppy seeds

1   tablespoon sugar

1   teaspoon kosher salt

½   teaspoon white pepper

MAKES 8 SERVINGS

In a large mixing bowl, combine all ingredients for salad. In a medium bowl, whisk together ingredients for dressing until well combined and emulsified. Toss dressing into slaw, taste for seasoning, and then refrigerate several hours before serving.

*You can use 1/2 head red cabbage shredded, 1/2 head green cabbage shredded, and 2 carrots, julienned or shredded instead of the prepared packages.

Five Herb, Heirloom Tomato, and Mozzarella Pasta Salad

1   pound imported pasta (penne, farfalle, or other tubular shaped pasta)

¼   cup each chopped fresh parsley, basil, oregano, mint, thyme

½   cup extra virgin olive oil

2   teaspoons kosher salt

1   teaspoon ground black pepper

2   to 3 large cloves garlic, minced

2   pounds heirloom or other flavorful tomatoes, coarsely chopped

1   pound fresh mozzarella, cut into 1-inch dice

½   cup shaved Parmesan cheese

MAKES 6 SERVINGS

Cook pasta *al dente*, drain, and place in a large mixing bowl. Add remaining ingredients; toss gently. Taste for seasoning. Refrigerate until ready to serve.

NOTE: This is the perfect summer fresh herb and tomato combination.

Fireworks Vegetable and Seafood Salad

1 carrot, julienned
1 (5-inch) piece of daikon (Japanese white radish), julienned
1 cup thinly sliced red cabbage
1 bunch green onions, thinly sliced on diagonal
½ pound crabmeat
½ pound bay scallops, poached for 30 seconds and drained
1 jalapeño pepper, cored and diced
¼ cup chopped fresh cilantro
1 large clove garlic, minced
2 teaspoons toasted sesame oil
1 teaspoon sugar
2 tablespoons vegetable or canola oil
2 tablespoons soy sauce
4 large leaves of butter or Bibb lettuce, washed and dried
2 tablespoons black sesame seeds (for garnish)

MAKES 4 SERVINGS

In a medium bowl, combine carrot and daikon. Toss in cabbage, onions, crabmeat, poached scallops, jalapeño, cilantro, garlic, sesame oil, sugar, vegetable or canola oil, and soy sauce. The recipe can be made several hours ahead up to this point. Place each of the lettuce leaves on a salad plate. Place one fourth of the filling in each of the lettuce leaves, and then sprinkle the sesame seeds on top.

Portobello Mushroom Salad

¼ cup extra virgin olive oil
1 large onion, thinly sliced
2 tablespoons minced garlic
4 large portobello mushrooms, stems removed, thinly sliced
1 red bell pepper, cored and thinly sliced
1 cup chopped fresh Italian parsley
Zest and juice of 1 lemon
2 tablespoons red wine vinegar
2 teaspoons kosher salt
1 teaspoon ground black pepper
4 ounces feta cheese

MAKES 4 SERVINGS

In a medium skillet, heat oil and sauté onion until soft. Add garlic and mushrooms, toss, and cook until mushrooms soften slightly, about 3 to 5 minutes. Place in a mixing bowl with bell pepper, parsley, lemon juice and zest, red wine vinegar, salt, and pepper. Toss gently. Place in a serving bowl; sprinkle with feta cheese.

Roasted Beet, Spinach, and Orange Salad

Roasted Beet, Spinach, and Orange Salad

SALAD

3   pounds fresh beets*
2   tablespoons olive oil
4 to 6 cups baby spinach leaves
4   ounces feta cheese, crumbled
½   cup toasted chopped hazelnuts

DRESSING

Zest of 2 large oranges (reserve the oranges for slicing in salad)
⅛   teaspoon cayenne pepper
¼   cup balsamic vinegar
2   cloves garlic, minced
1   teaspoon kosher salt
½   teaspoon ground black pepper
½   cup extra virgin olive oil

MAKES 4 SERVINGS

Wash beets; trim the ends and remove the greens. Rub beets with oil, place in aluminum foil, tightly wrap, and put on a baking sheet. Roast in a preheated oven at 400 degrees F for 1 hour. Remove from oven, open foil package, and cool slightly. Under cold water, remove the skins of the beets (wear plastic gloves to prevent staining hands). Thinly slice the beets and place in a medium bowl. Wash the spinach leaves and pat dry with paper towels. Arrange the spinach leaves on a decorative platter. Top with sliced beets, feta cheese, and hazelnuts. Slice the reserved oranges and arrange around perimeter of platter. Drizzle with dressing just before serving.

In a bowl, whisk together all ingredients for dressing. This can be done a day ahead.

*I like using a combination of red, yellow, and striped, if available.

Shrimp, Asparagus, and Strawberry Salad

SALAD

1   pound jumbo raw shrimp (16 to 21 per pound), peeled and deveined
2   tablespoons extra virgin olive oil
1/2 teaspoon paprika
2   large cloves garlic, minced
1/4 cup chopped fresh parsley
Juice and zest of 1 lemon
1   bunch fresh asparagus, ends trimmed and cut into 2-inch pieces
1   red bell pepper, cored and chopped
6   cups baby arugula leaves
1/2 cup coarsely chopped fresh mint leaves
8   large strawberries, cut in half lengthwise

DRESSING

Zest and juice of 1 large or 2 small oranges
1   large clove garlic, minced
1   teaspoon dried dill weed
1   teaspoon kosher salt
1/2 teaspoon ground black pepper
1/2 cup toasted pine nuts
4   ounces feta cheese
Fresh mint leaves (for garnish)
Lemon slices (for garnish)

MAKES 4 SERVINGS

In a medium bowl, combine the shrimp, oil, paprika, garlic, parsley, and lemon juice and zest. Marinate for 1 to 2 hours, if time allows. Heat a grill pan or use an outdoor grill with a barbeque basket. Remove shrimp from marinade and cook over medium-high heat until shrimp are pink, about 3 to 4 minutes, tossing often to cook evenly. Set aside.

Blanch asparagus for 2 minutes in boiling salted water to which 1 tablespoon of oil has been added. Drain; cool. In a bowl, combine the asparagus, bell pepper, arugula, and mint. Arrange on a decorative platter. Place sliced strawberries and shrimp on arugula mixture.

In a small bowl, whisk orange zest and juice, garlic, dill, salt, and pepper. Drizzle over salad just before serving. Top with the pine nuts and feta cheese, and garnish with mint and lemon.

Shrimp, Asparagus, and Strawberry Salad

Two Melon and Cucumber Mint Salad

Two Melon and Cucumber Mint Salad

6   cups 1-inch cubed seedless watermelon
1   small cantaloupe, cut into 1-inch cubes
1   English cucumber, thinly sliced
½   cup chopped fresh mint leaves
Juice and zest of 2 limes
½   jalapeño pepper, cored and diced
Pinch kosher salt
2   tablespoons canola oil

MAKES 6 TO 8 SERVINGS

In a bowl, combine all ingredients and toss well. Allow to chill in the refrigerator for 1 hour before serving.

NOTE: A perfect summer salad to serve with grilled chicken or fish. Can be served alone as a main course with crusty bread and sliced cheeses.

Seafood

THE RECIPES

Calamari with Fingerling Potatoes and Fennel

CALAMARI

3 tablespoons extra virgin olive oil
2 cloves garlic, minced
1 pound cleaned raw calamari, rings and tentacles, patted dry with paper towels

POTATOES

3   tablespoons extra virgin olive oil
2   pounds fingerling potatoes, cut in half lengthwise
1   bulb fennel, outer layer and fronds removed, thinly sliced
¼   pound pitted kalamata olives
⅛   teaspoon red pepper flakes
½   teaspoon kosher salt
1   cup chopped fresh sage leaves

MAKES 4 SERVINGS

Heat the olive oil in medium sauté pan. Add the garlic and calamari; sauté for 2 minutes over medium-high heat. Transfer to a mixing bowl.

In a separate bowl, combine 3 tablespoons oil, potatoes, fennel, olives, and red pepper flakes. Place in single layer in a medium roasting pan. Bake in a preheated oven at 375 degrees F for 20 minutes, tossing once during the cooking process. Add the potatoes to the calamari along with salt and sage, and then toss. Serve at once.

Gratin of Crabmeat and Artichokes

6   tablespoons butter, divided
1   medium onion, chopped
1   bunch green onions, thinly sliced
½   cup all-purpose flour
1½ cups whole milk or half-and-half
¼   teaspoon paprika
½   teaspoon kosher salt
½   cup grated Parmesan cheese
1   pound crabmeat
½   pound sliced mushrooms
1   can (15 ounces) artichoke hearts, drained and chopped
1   cup plain dry bread crumbs

MAKES 6 SERVINGS

In a medium sauté pan, heat 2 tablespoons butter and sauté the onion and green onions for 3 minutes until softened. Stir in the flour; cook for 1 minute, stirring often. Whisk in milk or half-and-half and cook on low for 2 to 3 minutes, whisking until thickened. Stir in paprika, salt, cheese, and crabmeat. Set aside.

In a small skillet, heat remaining butter and sauté mushrooms for 3 minutes. Add to skillet with crabmeat and then stir in artichokes hearts. Pour entire mixture into a 2-quart greased baking dish. Top with bread crumbs.

Bake in a preheated oven at 350 degrees F for 15 minutes. Serve at once with sliced French bread on the side.

Calamari with Fingerling Potatoes and Fennel

Crab and Chipotle Onion Quesadillas

1   large sweet onion (such as Maui, Mayan, Vidalia, or Walla Walla), thinly sliced

3 to 4 tablespoons vegetable oil, divided

2   chipotle peppers in adobo (from a 7-ounce can), finely chopped

1   cup sour cream

1/2   pound crabmeat

2   green onions, thinly sliced on diagonal

1/2   cup chopped fresh cilantro

2   cups grated Monterey Jack cheese

10   (8-inch) flour tortillas

MAKES 20 WEDGES

In a skillet, sauté onion in 1 tablespoon oil until softened and slightly golden, about 3 to 4 minutes. Add the chopped chipotle peppers and cook another 2 minutes. Remove from heat, add the sour cream, and stir until combined. Set aside.

In a small bowl, combine the crabmeat, green onions, cilantro, and cheese. Mix well. Place 5 tortillas on a work surface and divide the onion-chipotle mixture among the tortillas; spread evenly. Top each of the tortillas equally with the crabmeat mixture. Place a second tortilla on top of each. Heat 1 tablespoon of oil in a 10-inch skillet, add one stuffed tortilla, and place a heavy pan on top of the tortilla to weigh it down. Cook for 2 minutes, turn, and cook another 1 to 2 minutes until golden brown. Remove from pan and cut into 4 wedges. Continue in the same manner with the remaining 4 quesadillas. Serve with Pico De Gallo (see page 98) and Classic Guacamole (see page 100).

Crispy Shrimp and Pork Wontons

FILLING

2   tablespoons peanut or vegetable oil
½   pound lean ground pork
1   pound raw shrimp, peeled and deveined, finely chopped
2   cloves garlic, minced
1   teaspoon Asian hot garlic chili paste
2   tablespoons soy sauce
1   tablespoon Chinese rice wine vinegar or pale dry sherry
1   teaspoon kosher salt
6   water chestnuts, finely chopped
1   green onion, finely chopped
1   teaspoon cornstarch dissolved in 1 tablespoon water

WRAPPERS

36   wonton wrappers
3   cups peanut oil

MAKES ABOUT 36 WONTONS

Heat a wok or skillet over high heat. Add oil; heat until smoking about 1 minute, and then add pork, shrimp, garlic, chili paste, soy sauce, vinegar or sherry, salt, water chestnuts, and green onion. Stir-fry until shrimp turn pink and pork is cooked through. Add cornstarch mixture and stir-fry until the filling thickens slightly; cool to room temperature.

Put the wonton wrappers on a work surface. Place 1 teaspoon filling in the center of each wonton wrapper. With a finger dipped in water, moisten the edges of the wrapper, and then bring one corner up over the filling to the opposite corner to form a triangle. Moisten and pull the two bottom corners of the folded triangle forward and under the wonton so the two edges meet and slightly overlap.

As each wonton is done, place it on a plate and cover with a dry towel. If the wontons must wait longer than 30 minutes before frying, cover with plastic wrap and refrigerate. When ready to fry, pour 3 cups peanut oil in a deep saucepan or fryer. Heat the oil until a haze forms or the oil reads 375 degrees F on a deep-fry thermometer. Deep fry the wontons, 4 to 6 at a time, for 2 minutes or until they are crisp and golden. Remove from oil with a slotted spoon or a "Chinese spider." Drain off excess oil on a platter lined with paper towels. Serve with Honey-Orange-Sesame Dipping Sauce (see page 102).

Feta and Herb Stuffed Shrimp

Feta and Herb Stuffed Shrimp

4   ounces crumbled feta cheese
4   ounces cream cheese, softened
1   tablespoon finely chopped fresh parsley
1   tablespoon finely chopped chives or green onions
1   large clove garlic, minced
¼   teaspoon kosher salt
¼   teaspoon ground black pepper
24 large raw shrimp, peeled and deveined
½   head red cabbage, shredded
4   cups spinach leaves
2   tablespoons balsamic vinegar (for garnish)
2   tablespoons finely chopped fresh parsley (for garnish)

MAKES 24 STUFFED SHRIMP

In a small bowl combine the feta cheese, cream cheese, parsley, chives or green onions, garlic, salt, and pepper. Mix well, using your hands to combine thoroughly.

Cut the shrimp along the back to "butterfly," cutting about 1/2 inch deep. Spread the shrimp open and stuff 1 teaspoon of the filling into each shrimp. Place shrimp on baking sheet, cheese side up. The recipe can be made several hours ahead up to this point.

Preheat broiler and broil the shrimp 6 inches from the heat source until the cheese is bubbly and the shrimp are pink, about 4 to 5 minutes. Remove from oven.

Place shredded cabbage and spinach leaves on a serving platter to make a bed of greens for the shrimp. Place cooked shrimp on the greens, cheese side up, and drizzle with balsamic vinegar and parsley.

Grilled Asian Salmon on Mixed Greens

SALMON

$\frac{1}{2}$ cup soy sauce
$\frac{1}{4}$ cup rice wine vinegar
2 tablespoons canola oil
$\frac{1}{4}$ cup honey or brown sugar
2 teaspoons grated fresh ginger
4 cloves garlic, minced
2 tablespoons sesame oil
4 (6-ounce) salmon fillets

GREENS

2 cups shredded matchstick carrots
1 bunch green onions, thinly sliced on diagonal
2 cups frozen green peas, thawed
8 cups mixed greens
Toasted sesame seeds (for garnish)

MAKES 4 SERVINGS

In a bowl, combine soy sauce, vinegar, canola oil, honey or brown sugar, ginger, garlic, and sesame oil. Whisk well. Marinate salmon in half the soy sauce marinade for at least 30 minutes and up to 2 hours; reserve the other half for later use. Heat a grill pan or large skillet; sear the salmon fillets for 4 to 5 minutes per side, depending on thickness.

In a large bowl, combine carrots, green onions, peas, and mixed greens. This can be done ahead of time. Toss in some of the reserved marinade, just enough to coat the lettuce slightly. Place greens on a large serving platter; top with grilled salmon fillets, and garnish with toasted sesame seeds.

NOTE: This recipe works well with grilled chicken also. Substitute 4 boneless and skinless chicken breasts for the salmon, marinate in same manner, then grill and thinly slice.

Grilled Salmon with Mushroom Pinot Noir Sauce

SALMON

¼ cup olive oil
1 cup chopped fresh Italian parsley
½ cup chopped fresh chives or green onions
1 teaspoon kosher salt
¼ teaspoon ground black pepper
½ teaspoon paprika
6 (4- to 6-ounce) salmon fillets

MUSHROOM PINOT NOIR SAUCE

6 tablespoons butter, divided
2 cloves garlic, minced
½ medium onion, chopped
4 cups fresh mushrooms (button, shiitake, crimini, etc., or a combination), thinly sliced
1 teaspoon dried thyme leaves
1 teaspoon kosher salt
¼ teaspoon ground white pepper
2 cups pinot noir or other mild-bodied red wine
2 tablespoons chopped fresh thyme leaves (for garnish)
¼ cup chopped fresh chives (for garnish)

MAKES 4 TO 6 SERVINGS

In a bowl, combine oil, parsley, chives or green onions, salt, pepper, and paprika. Dip each salmon fillet into the mixture and set aside while heating a grill pan over medium heat for 2 to 3 minutes. Grill each fillet for 4 to 5 minutes per side. Place on serving platter.

In a skillet, heat 4 tablespoons butter and sauté garlic for 30 seconds. Add onion and mushrooms; sauté until softened, about 3 minutes. Add thyme, salt, pepper, and pinot noir or other red wine. Cook uncovered for 3 to 5 minutes until slightly thickened. Stir in remaining butter. Cook 1 minute more. Pour over salmon. Serve at once with chopped fresh thyme or chives on top.

NOTE: This dish is excellent served with Parslied Potatoes and Parsnips Parmesan (see page 184).

Gazpacho Crabmeat Martini

GAZPACHO

2 medium cucumbers, peeled, seeded, and coarsely chopped
½ green pepper, cored and chopped
¼ cup red onion, coarsely chopped
4 tomatoes, cored and chopped
¼ cup chopped fresh cilantro leaves
1 cup chopped Romaine lettuce
1 clove garlic, chopped
Juice of 2 limes
1 teaspoon kosher salt
¼ cup extra virgin olive oil

CRAB

½ pound fresh crabmeat
¼ cup chopped fresh chives (for garnish)
6 lime slices (for garnish)

MAKES 6 TO 8 SERVINGS

Place all ingredients for Gazpacho in a food processor and pulse on and off until chunky, not pureed. If it is too thick, add a little water. Transfer to large bowl and refrigerate at least 2 hours. When ready to serve, divide the Gazpacho among 6 martini glasses or decorative goblets. Top each with a heaping tablespoon of crabmeat and garnish with chives and a slice of lime.

Margarita Shrimp

2 pounds large cooked shrimp, thawed if frozen
1 teaspoon sugar
1 jalapeño pepper, cored and diced
½ cup tequila
1 cup chopped fresh cilantro
1 teaspoon kosher salt
1 lime, thinly sliced (for garnish)
Zest and juice of 2 limes
Zest and juice of 1 large or 2 small oranges
Cilantro leaves (for garnish)
Strips of orange zest* (for garnish)

MAKES 6 SERVINGS

In a medium bowl, combine all ingredients. Toss well; marinate for at least 1 hour and up to 4 hours. Serve with toothpicks in an oversized margarita glass or decorative glass bowl. Garnish with lime, cilantro, and orange zest.

*Use a scorer to get thin strips of zest.

Gazpacho Crabmeat Martini

Salmon Cakes with Lemon Aioli

SALMON CAKES

2	cups cooked salmon, flaked
1/2	cup dry bread crumbs
2	green onions, chopped
1/4	cup diced celery
1/4	cup mayonnaise
1/8	teaspoon cayenne pepper
1	teaspoon dried dill
1	teaspoon dried thyme
1	teaspoon Worcestershire sauce
1	egg
1/2	teaspoon kosher salt
2	tablespoons butter
1	tablespoon canola or vegetable oil

2 to 4 cups mixed greens, leaf lettuce, Bibb lettuce, or radicchio (for serving)

Fresh dill sprigs or parsley sprigs (for garnish)

Chopped green onions (for garnish)

LEMON AIOLI

1/2	cup mayonnaise
2	tablespoons cream

Zest and juice of 1 lemon

1	tablespoon prepared horseradish
1	teaspoon chopped fresh garlic
1	teaspoon dried thyme

MAKES 4 SERVINGS (2 EACH)

In a bowl, combine the salmon, bread crumbs, green onions, celery, mayonnaise, cayenne pepper, dill, thyme, Worcestershire sauce, egg, and salt. Shape into 8 salmon cakes. Melt butter and oil in a heavy skillet. Brown salmon cakes on both sides, about 5 minutes per side. Place on a serving platter lined with mixed greens, leaf lettuce, Bibb lettuce, or radicchio. Top each with a dollop of Lemon Aioli and garnish with dill or parsley and green onions.

To make the Lemon Aioli, combine the mayonnaise, cream, lemon zest and juice, horseradish, garlic, and thyme. Mix well; refrigerate until ready to serve.

Sea Scallop Skewers with Gremolata (Parsley-Lemon Sauce)

SEA SCALLOPS

2 pounds sea scallops (about 32 scallops)
¼ cup extra virgin olive oil
Zest and juice of 1 lemon
2 cloves garlic, minced
1 bunch green onions, thinly sliced
½ teaspoon paprika
¼ cup chopped fresh parsley
¼ cup chopped fresh mint leaves
10 to 12 (10-inch) heavy duty wooden skewers

GREMOLATA

1 cup chopped Italian parsley
Zest and juice of 1 lemon
2 garlic cloves, minced
2 tablespoons extra virgin olive oil
½ teaspoon kosher salt
¼ teaspoon ground black pepper

MAKES ABOUT 10 TO 12 SKEWERS

In a medium bowl, combine the scallops, oil, lemon zest and juice, garlic, green onions, paprika, parsley, and mint. Marinate for 1 to 2 hours. Soak wooden skewers in water for 10 minutes to prevent them burning on the grill. Thread 3 to 4 scallops on each skewer. Heat an outdoor grill to medium, heat a grill pan over medium-high heat, or use a broiler. Cook the skewers for 2 to 3 minutes, turn, and cook the other side. Transfer to serving platter.

For the Gremolata, combine parsley, lemon zest and juice, garlic, olive oil, salt, and pepper in a small mixing bowl. Spread each cooked skewer with a teaspoon of Gremolata.

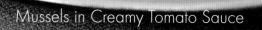
Mussels in Creamy Tomato Sauce

Mussels in Creamy Tomato Sauce

3 pounds fresh black mussels, cleaned and debearded
2 tablespoons butter
2 tablespoons olive oil
2 large shallots, chopped
2 cloves garlic, slivered
½ cup chopped fresh parsley
1 teaspoon dried thyme
4 Roma tomatoes, chopped
1 cup white wine
1 cup heavy cream

MAKES 4 SERVINGS

Place cleaned mussels in a bowl and set aside. In a large saucepan, heat butter and oil. Sauté shallots for 1 minute. Add garlic, parsley, and thyme. Cook another minute. Add tomatoes, wine, and mussels. Cover and cook for 5 to 7 minutes over medium-high heat until mussels have opened. Stir in cream. Cook another minute over low heat, but do not allow to boil. Remove and discard any unopened mussels at this time.

NOTE: Serve as an appetizer with crusty bread or pour sauce over prepared linguine and serve as a meal.

Seafood-Stuffed Endive Spears

½ pound crabmeat
½ pound bay shrimp
¼ cup finely diced red bell pepper
¼ cup finely diced celery
2 tablespoons finely chopped red onion
2 tablespoons finely chopped Italian parsley
½ cup mayonnaise
1 teaspoon lemon pepper seasoning
1 teaspoon dried dill weed
2 to 3 heads Belgian endive (red or white)*
Zest of 2 lemons (for garnish)
¼ cup chopped fresh Italian parsley (for garnish)

MAKES ABOUT 32 SPEARS

In a bowl, combine all ingredients except endive and garnishes. Place the endive leaves (and/or radicchio leaves if using) on a large serving platter in a concentric circle. Place a teaspoon of filling in each of the leaves. Garnish with lemon zest and parsley. Serve chilled. This recipe can be made several hours ahead.

*You can also use 1 head radicchio, leaves separated, or a combination of endive and radicchio leaves.

Sesame Shrimp with Spicy Thai Dipping Sauce

SESAME SHRIMP

2   pounds large cooked shrimp
1   teaspoon sesame oil
¼   cup soy sauce
1   cup chopped fresh cilantro leaves
¼   cup chopped fresh mint leaves
1   tablespoon grated fresh gingerroot
2   teaspoons sugar
Juice of 2 limes
4   small dried red chile peppers, cut in half
¼   cup toasted sesame seeds

SPICY THAI DIPPING SAUCE

½   cup Asian fish sauce
Juice of 2 limes
1   teaspoon Asian hot garlic chili paste
1   tablespoon chopped fresh cilantro leaves
2   tablespoons vegetable oil
1   teaspoon sugar
1   garlic clove, minced

MAKES 8 SERVINGS (6 EACH)

In a bowl, combine shrimp, sesame oil, soy sauce, cilantro, mint, ginger, sugar, lime juice, and chile peppers. Toss well; marinate for at least 2 hours. Remove the shrimp from the marinade and place on a decorative platter. Discard marinade. Sprinkle shrimp with toasted sesame seeds.

In a bowl, whisk together all the ingredients for the Spicy Thai Dipping Sauce. Serve on the side for dipping.

Shrimp and Rice Stuffed Artichokes

ARTICHOKES

2	large artichokes
4	cups chicken broth
4	cups water
1	tablespoon kosher salt

FILLING

1/2	pound peeled and cooked shrimp, coarsely chopped
1	cup cooked rice*
1/2	cup frozen peas, thawed
1/2	cup thinly sliced celery
1/2	red bell pepper, cored and chopped

DRESSING

	Zest and juice of 1 lemon
2	tablespoons olive oil
2	tablespoons mayonnaise
1/4	cup chopped Italian parsley
1	teaspoon dried dill weed
1	teaspoon kosher salt
1/2	teaspoon ground black pepper

GARNISH

Chopped fresh parsley
Lemon zest

MAKES 2 SERVINGS

Clean artichokes, trim tops and ends, and remove tough outer leaves. In a medium saucepan, bring broth, water, and salt to a boil. Add artichokes, lower heat to a simmer, cover, and cook for 45 minutes until tender. When artichokes are cooked, remove from liquid, cool slightly, and then remove the center "choke" with a serrated spoon or sharp grapefruit knife.

For the filling, combine shrimp, rice, peas, celery, and bell pepper in a medium bowl. Set aside.

Whisk together all ingredients for the dressing in a small bowl. Pour dressing over rice mixture; mix well. Fill the center of each artichoke with shrimp filling and sprinkle with parsley and lemon zest to garnish.

*Long grain works well.

Seared Salmon with Leek-Carrot Sauce

SALMON

4   (6- to 8-ounce) salmon fillets
2   tablespoons olive oil
Kosher salt to taste
Ground black pepper to taste
Paprika to taste

LEEK-CARROT SAUCE

2   tablespoons butter
1   leek, white part only, washed and thinly sliced or julienned
2   carrots, julienned
1   cup white wine
1   teaspoon thyme leaves
½   teaspoon kosher salt
⅛   teaspoon ground white pepper
Corn-Tomato-Mint Salsa (see page 98)

MAKES 4 SERVINGS

Place salmon on a work surface; brush both sides with oil. Sprinkle both sides with salt, pepper, and paprika. Heat a 12-inch nonstick skillet over medium-high heat for 2 minutes. Place salmon in pan and cook for 5 minutes per side. This will create a crusty outer surface on the salmon. (Salmon should be crispy on outside and medium on the inside.) Remove salmon from pan; add butter, leeks, and carrots and cook for 2 minutes until softened. Add wine, thyme, salt, and pepper; cook 1 or 2 more minutes until the sauce has thickened slightly. Put a bed of Corn-Tomato-Mint Salsa on a serving platter. Lay salmon on the salsa and pour Leek-Carrot Sauce over the salmon.

Seared Salmon with Leek-Carrot Sauce

Seared Scallop Salad with Almond-Cucumber Dressing

SALAD

1 pound large scallops, patted dry with paper towels to remove excess liquid (about 16 to 18 scallops)
2 tablespoons olive oil
½ cup chopped fresh parsley
½ cup chopped fresh tarragon
1 teaspoon kosher salt
½ teaspoon ground black pepper
4 cups spring mix or spinach leaves

ALMOND-CUCUMBER DRESSING

½ cup olive oil
2 tablespoons chopped fresh tarragon
1 teaspoon kosher salt
½ teaspoon ground black pepper
1 cup toasted slivered almonds
1 cucumber, thinly sliced
Juice and zest of 1 lemon

MAKES 4 SERVINGS

In a bowl, combine scallops, oil, parsley, tarragon, salt, and pepper. Heat a grill pan or sauté pan for 2 minutes over medium-high heat to ensure the scallops will sear. Add the scallops, a few at a time so as not to crowd the pan. Grill for 3 minutes per side. Remove to a platter lined with spring mix or spinach leaves.

In a bowl, whisk together lemon zest and juice, oil, tarragon, salt, and pepper. Stir in almonds and cucumber. Pour over the scallops and serve at once.

Mediterranean Shrimp Bundles with Lemon Mint Rice

4   sheets parchment paper (14 x 14 inches), each cut into a heart shape
1   pound raw jumbo shrimp, peeled and deveined
2   large Roma tomatoes, cored and chopped
1   large clove garlic, minced
2   tablespoons olive oil
$1/4$ cup chopped fresh oregano or 1 tablespoon dried oregano
1   teaspoon salt
$1/2$ teaspoon ground black pepper
4   ounces crumbled feta cheese
Lemon Mint Rice (see page 92)

MAKES 4 SERVINGS

Place each sheet of parchment paper on a work surface. Fold in half to make a crease down center of the heart shape. Place 5 shrimp on one half of each of the paper hearts.

In a small bowl, mix together tomatoes, garlic, oil, oregano, salt, pepper, and feta cheese. Divide the tomato mixture among the four paper hearts and place on top of the shrimp.

Fold over the parchment paper to form an "envelope" and secure the ends by crimping and folding the paper. Place each bundle on a baking sheet and bake at 375 degrees F for 8 to 10 minutes. This recipe can be assembled ahead of time, and then baked just before serving. After baking, remove from oven, cut open the package, and serve with Lemon Mint Rice.

Skewered Salmon in Sesame Sauce

Skewered Salmon in Sesame Sauce

SALMON

2 to 3 pounds skinless salmon fillets
30 to 36 (6-inch) wooden skewers

SESAME SAUCE

2   tablespoons canola or peanut oil
1   teaspoon Chinese Five Spice
1   tablespoon toasted sesame oil
1   teaspoon kosher salt
½   teaspoon ground black pepper
¼   cup chopped fresh mint leaves
¼   cup chopped fresh cilantro
2   tablespoons toasted sesame seeds

MAKES ABOUT 30 TO 36 SKEWERS

Cut the salmon fillets crosswise, against the grain, into 1 x 3 inch strips. There should be about 30 strips. Place in a medium glass or ceramic bowl.

In a separate bowl, whisk ingredients for Sesame Sauce together. Pour over the salmon strips and allow the fish to marinate in refrigerator for at least 1 hour and up to 4 hours. Soak the wooden skewers in water for 10 minutes. Thread one strip of salmon onto a skewer. Repeat until all the salmon has been skewered. Place skewers on a baking sheet in a single layer, drizzle any remaining marinade over salmon, and bake in a preheated oven at 375 degrees F for 5 to 8 minutes, until cooked through.

NOTE: Serve with Honey-Orange-Sesame Dipping Sauce (see page 102), Mango-Avocado Salsa (see page 98), or Grilled Peach and Red Pepper Salsa (see page 100). You can substitute strips of chicken, beef, or raw large shrimp for the salmon.

Walnut-Crusted Halibut on Wilted Greens

HALIBUT

½   cup finely chopped walnuts
2   cups soft bread crumbs (made with day old bread)
2   tablespoons melted butter
1   teaspoon dried dill weed
½   cup chopped fresh parsley
Juice of 1 lemon
1   teaspoon kosher salt
¼   teaspoon coarse ground black pepper
4   (6-ounce) halibut fillets*
2   teaspoons olive oil
1   lemon, thinly sliced (for garnish)

WILTED GREENS

2   tablespoons olive oil
3   cloves garlic, cut into thin slivers
4   cups spinach leaves
1   bunch Swiss chard or kale, cleaned and coarsely chopped
¼   teaspoon grated nutmeg
1   teaspoon kosher salt

MAKES 4 SERVINGS

In a small bowl, combine walnuts, bread crumbs, butter, dill, parsley, lemon juice, salt, and pepper. Place fish fillets on a baking sheet. Divide the breadcrumb mixture evenly over the 4 fillets, then spread and press down the crumb layer. Drizzle with oil and bake in preheated oven at 375 degrees F for 10 minutes.

In a large skillet, heat oil and sauté garlic until fragrant, about 1 minute over medium heat. Add spinach and chard or kale, nutmeg, and salt. Cover and cook 3 to 4 minutes, stirring often until greens are wilted. Serve halibut on wilted greens with lemon slices on the side.

*Salmon, red snapper, or tilapia fillets may be substituted.

Zucchini and Two-Potato Pancakes with Smoked Salmon

TWO-POTATO PANCAKES

1	medium zucchini, julienned or grated
1	medium yam, peeled and julienned or grated
1	large russet potato, peeled and julienned or grated
2	tablespoons grated onion
¼	cup flour
2	large eggs
1	teaspoon salt
¼	teaspoon ground white pepper
1	teaspoon dried dill weed
2	tablespoons vegetable oil

SALMON

4	ounces smoked salmon (lox), thinly sliced
1	cup sour cream
¼	cup finely chopped chives
1	ounce domestic caviar (optional)

MAKES ABOUT 10 TO 12 SERVINGS

Place julienned or grated zucchini, yam, potato, and onion in a clean kitchen towel and twist to get out excess water.

In a bowl, whisk together flour, eggs, salt, pepper, and dill. Add the vegetables and stir well. Heat oil in 12-inch skillet. Add a heaping table-spoonful of potato mixture to hot oil, spreading out evenly; cook over medium heat for 2 to 3 minutes, turn, and cook another minute on other side. Transfer to a plate lined with paper towels. Repeat this process until all the potato mixture is used (about 10 to 12 pancakes).

Place pancakes on a serving platter. Top each with a thin slice of smoked salmon, a dollop of sour cream, chives, and 1/2 teaspoon caviar if using. Serve at once.

Pacific Northwest Rubbed Salmon on Cedar

SALMON

2 to 2½ pounds side of salmon, cut into 5 or 6 (6-ounce) fillets
1 tablespoon brown sugar
1 teaspoon dried thyme
1 teaspoon dried dill
¼ teaspoon paprika
1 teaspoon fennel seeds
1 teaspoon ground cumin
½ teaspoon ground cinnamon

CEDAR PLANK GRILLING

1 cedar plank for cooking (12 x 6 inches)*
1 large onion, thinly sliced
1 fennel bulb, thinly sliced

MAKES 5 TO 6 SERVINGS

Place salmon fillets on a work surface. In a bowl, combine sugar, thyme, dill, paprika, fennel seeds, cumin, and cinnamon. Rub all sides of salmon with this mixture; allow to "cure" by chilling in the refrigerator at least 30 minutes and up to 4 hours.

Place cedar plank in water to soak for 30 minutes. Remove from water and line plank with sliced onions and fennel. Place the seasoned salmon on the vegetables (skin side down if there is skin on the salmon) on the plank and grill over low heat, with grill lid down, for 15 to 20 minutes or until salmon is cooked. There is no need to turn the salmon over. Remove plank from grill; serve salmon from the cedar plank and then discard the plank.

NOTE: If you do not have a cedar plank for grilling, heat a regular grill to medium. Place salmon on grill, cover, and cook for 4 to 5 minutes per side, depending on thickness of salmon.

*This can be found in specialty food stores, supermarkets, or gourmet stores.

Sesame-Coated Tuna with Wasabi Mayonnaise

TUNA

1   pound sushi-quality tuna steaks, cut 1 inch thick
2   tablespoons olive oil
1   tablespoon toasted sesame oil
¼   cup white sesame seeds
¼   cup black sesame seeds
1   teaspoon kosher salt
1   teaspoon ground black pepper
½   head red cabbage, thinly sliced

WASABI MAYONNAISE

1   teaspoon wasabi powder*
¼   cup mayonnaise
2 to 3 tablespoons heavy cream

MAKES 4 SERVINGS

Place tuna steaks on a work surface. Mix olive oil and sesame oil in a bowl. Brush both sides of tuna with oil mixture. In another bowl, combine sesame seeds, salt, and pepper. Dredge each side of tuna in sesame seed mixture; set aside. Heat a nonstick skillet over high heat for 1 minute. Add tuna and cook for 2 minutes per side. Transfer to serving platter. Cut against the grain into thin strips. Place slices on shredded cabbage and drizzle with Wasabi Mayonnaise.

Combine all ingredients for Wasabi Mayonnaise in a bowl. It should be the consistency of thick heavy cream. This can be made ahead and refrigerated.

NOTE: The tuna should be rare, thinly sliced, and served slightly warm, not hot.

*You can use more if you like it "hot."

Soups and Stews

THE RECIPES

Louisiana Sweet Potato and Sausage Stew

STEW

3   tablespoons olive oil
1   large onion, chopped
1   red bell pepper, cored and chopped
1   orange bell pepper, cored and chopped
4   ribs celery, thinly sliced on diagonal
1   pound boneless and skinless chicken or turkey breasts, cut into 1-inch pieces
1   pound (about 4 links) andouille, polish kielbasa, or other spicy sausage, cut into 1-inch pieces
2   large cloves garlic, minced
1   teaspoon cumin powder
1   teaspoon paprika
1   teaspoon chili powder
1   can (4 ounces) chopped green chiles
1   can (15 ounces) garbanzo beans, with liquid
1   can (15 ounces) chopped tomatoes, with liquid
1   can (15 ounces) water (use empty chopped tomato can to measure)
4   cups peeled and diced sweet potatoes
1   teaspoon kosher salt

GARNISHES

1   bunch fresh cilantro, coarsely chopped
1   cup sour cream
1   bunch green onions, thinly sliced

In a large stockpot, heat oil and sauté onion, bell peppers, and celery until soft, about 3 minutes. Add chicken or turkey breast pieces, sausages, garlic, cumin, paprika, and chili powder. Cook over medium heat for 5 to 8 minutes, stirring to coat meat with spices and allowing chicken to brown on all sides. Add chiles, garbanzo beans, tomatoes, water, sweet potatoes, and salt. Cover and simmer on low heat for 30 minutes, stirring often to prevent stew from sticking to the bottom of the pan. Taste for seasoning. Serve in bowls. Put garnishes in separate bowls for diners to pick and choose toppings.

Louisiana Sweet Potato and Sausage Stew

French-Canadian Onion Soup

4 large sweet onions (such as Walla Walla, Mayan, Vidalia, or Maui), thinly sliced

6 tablespoons butter

4 tablespoons flour

1 teaspoon kosher salt

½ teaspoon ground black pepper

4 cloves garlic, minced

1 tablespoon sugar

¼ cup chopped fresh parsley

2 teaspoons dried thyme leaves

5 to 6 cups beef stock

2 cups dry white wine

8 slices French bread, cut 1 inch thick

1 cup grated Parmesan cheese

1 cup grated mozzarella cheese

2 tablespoons brandy

¼ cup grated Parmesan cheese (for garnish)

MAKES 8 SERVINGS

In a large stockpot, sauté onions in butter until golden brown, about 10 minutes. Add flour, salt, pepper, garlic, and sugar and cook over medium heat about 5 minutes, stirring often. Add parsley, thyme, stock, and wine; simmer for 30 minutes, covered.

While soup is cooking, toast French bread under broiler with Parmesan and mozzarella on top, until cheese is melted. Just before ready to serve, add brandy to soup; stir well. Taste for seasoning. Place a slice of toasted bread on the bottom of a soup bowl. Top with soup and serve at once with additional cheese on top.

Mushroom and Beef Barley Stew

2   tablespoons olive oil
2   leeks, white part only, thinly sliced
2   large portobello mushrooms, stems removed, chopped
1   pound roast beef (from deli section of supermarket), cut into ½-inch dice
8   cups beef broth
1   teaspoon dried thyme leaves
1   teaspoon fennel seeds
1   teaspoon kosher salt
½   teaspoon ground black pepper
2   cups barley, precooked in 4 cups water for 10 minutes, drained
1   bunch green onions, thinly sliced

MAKES 6 SERVINGS

In a medium saucepan, heat oil. Sauté leeks and mushrooms for 5 minutes, stirring often. Add roast beef, broth, thyme, fennel seeds, salt, pepper, and precooked barley. Cover and simmer for 30 minutes. Taste for seasoning. Serve in large soup bowls topped with sliced green onions.

Pork and Tomato Tortilla Soup with Avocado

Pork and Tomato Tortilla Soup with Avocado

SOUP

2 tablespoons extra virgin olive oil
1 large onion, chopped
2 large cloves garlic, minced
1 jalapeño pepper, cored and diced
1/4 New Mexico dried chili pepper or 1 teaspoon ground ancho chile pepper
1 tablespoon chili powder
1 tablespoon ground cumin
1 pound boneless pork loin, cut into 1-inch pieces
6 cups chicken or beef broth
1 can (28 ounces) chopped tomatoes
1½ teaspoons kosher salt
1 package (16 ounces) frozen corn kernels

TORTILLAS

8 corn tortillas, cut into 1/4-inch thin strips
Nonstick cooking spray
1 teaspoon chili powder

GARNISH

½ cup chopped fresh cilantro leaves
1 large avocado, peeled and cut into small dice
1 cup queso fresco, crumbled*
2 limes, quartered

MAKES 8 SERVINGS

In a large stockpot, heat oil and sauté onion until softened. Add garlic and jalapeño pepper, sautéing for 1 minute over low heat. Add dried chili pepper or ground chile pepper, chili powder, and cumin. Add pork loin pieces; stir to coat pork and cook until golden brown. Add broth, tomatoes, and salt. Cover; simmer for 1 hour, stirring occasionally. Add corn and cook for 5 more minutes. Taste for seasoning.

While soup is cooking, place tortillas strips on a 12 x 9-inch baking sheet in a single layer. Spray the tortillas with cooking spray, sprinkle with chili powder, and bake in an oven at 400 degrees F for 10 minutes or until crispy, tossing once.

To serve, place soup in individual bowls and top with cilantro, avocado, and queso fresco. Squeeze a lime wedge into each bowl of soup and top with tortilla strips.

*This is a Mexican cheese found in the specialty cheese section of the supermarket.

Italian Lentil Stew with Sausage

2   tablespoons extra virgin olive oil
1   medium onion, chopped
2   large cloves garlic, minced
1   carrot, peeled and chopped
2   ribs celery, chopped
1   green bell pepper, cored and chopped
2   cups brown lentils
6   cups water, vegetable broth, or chicken stock
1   tablespoon kosher salt
1   teaspoon ground black pepper
1   tablespoon dried Italian seasoning
1   cup dried ditalini or other small pasta
6   cups water (for cooking pasta)
1   teaspoon kosher salt
1   teaspoon oil
4   links (about 1 pound) Italian sausages
¼   cup grated Romano or Parmesan cheese

MAKES 4 SERVINGS

In a large stockpot, heat oil. Add onion; cook for 2 minutes. Add garlic, carrot, celery, and bell pepper. Cook another 2 to 3 minutes. Add lentils. Add water, vegetable broth, or chicken stock. Add salt, pepper, and Italian seasoning. Cover and simmer for 30 minutes.

In a 4-quart saucepan, cook pasta until *al dente* in 6 cups of boiling water with salt and oil added; drain. Add cooked pasta to lentils and cook another 5 minutes. Taste for seasoning.

In a medium skillet, cook sausages until browned on all sides. Add a little water, cover, and cook for 15 additional minutes.

To serve, place stew in four serving bowls. Cut slits in sausage 1 inch apart, and place one sausage atop each bowl of stew. Top with grated cheese. Serve at once.

Roasted Tomato and Basil Soup

16 Roma tomatoes, cored and cut in
   half horizontally
3 to 4 cloves garlic, slivered
2 to 3 tablespoons olive oil
1 tablespoon kosher salt
1 teaspoon ground black pepper
1 cup fresh basil leaves
2 cups beef, vegetable, or chicken
   broth
Juice of 1 lemon
1 tablespoon sugar
1/2 cup shaved Parmesan or Romano
   cheese
Salt and pepper to taste

MAKES 6 TO 8 SERVINGS

Place cut tomatoes, skin side down, on a baking sheet. Sprinkle with garlic, oil, salt, and pepper. Roast in a preheated oven at 400 degrees F for 25 minutes. Remove from oven; place tomatoes and garlic, with juices, in a food processor. Add basil, broth, lemon juice, sugar, and salt and pepper to taste. Pulse on and off until coarsely chopped, not pureed. (Or you can use an immersion blender in a large stockpot). Place the soup in a stockpot and bring to a simmer; cook for 5 minutes, stirring often. Serve warm or cold, with shaved cheese on top.

Spicy Corn and Crab Chowder

Roasted Pepper, Potato, and Leek Soup

4   tablespoons butter
1   large or 2 medium leeks, white part only, cleaned and thinly sliced
2   cloves garlic, minced
3   large russet potatoes, peeled and cut into 1-inch cubes
6 to 7 cups chicken or vegetable broth, divided
1   cup chopped Italian parsley
1   tablespoon kosher salt
½   teaspoon ground white pepper
1½   cups roasted red bell peppers (from a can or jar)
2   cups half-and-half
¼   cup chopped fresh chives

MAKES 4 TO 6 SERVINGS

In a medium saucepan, heat butter and sauté leeks for 3 to 4 minutes over medium heat, until soft. Add garlic. Sauté 1 minute more. Add potatoes, 4 cups broth, parsley, salt, and pepper. Cover and simmer for 15 to 20 minutes until potatoes are tender. Add peppers, half-and-half, and 2 to 3 more cups broth.

Cover and simmer another 2 to 3 minutes. Place soup in blender in small portions or use an immersion blender to puree. Taste for seasoning. Serve hot or cold, with sprinkle of fresh chives on top.

Spicy Corn and Crab Chowder

4   tablespoons butter
1   small onion, chopped
2   ribs celery, chopped
1   large russet potato, peeled and cut into ½-inch dice
1   jalapeño pepper, cored and finely diced
½   cup flour
16   ounces (2 8-ounce bottles) clam juice
2   cups half-and-half
2   cups whole milk
1   teaspoon Cajun or Creole seasoning
2   teaspoons kosher salt
½   pound crab or lobster meat
1   cup chopped cilantro
1   package (16 ounces) frozen corn kernels, thawed
Chopped cilantro leaves (for garnish)

MAKES 4 TO 6 SERVINGS

In a medium saucepan, heat butter. Sauté onion and celery until soft, about 2 to 3 minutes. Add potato and jalapeño pepper. Cook over low heat, covered, for 3 to 4 minutes, until potato is tender. Add flour; stir 1 minute. Stir in clam juice, half-and-half, milk, seasoning, and salt. Whisk together. Cover and simmer for 10 minutes over low heat, whisking often to prevent lumps. Stir in the crabmeat or lobster, cilantro, and corn. Cook over low heat for 2 minutes. Taste for seasoning. Ladle in soup bowls and garnish with cilantro.

Southwestern Chicken and Corn Stew

4	tablespoons vegetable or canola oil
1	large onion, diced
2	cloves garlic, minced
1	pound boneless and skinless chicken breasts, cut into 1-inch pieces
2	jalapeño peppers, cored and finely chopped
1	tablespoon chili powder
1	tablespoon ground cumin
1	tablespoon ground coriander
1	teaspoon kosher salt
1/4	teaspoon ground black pepper
1/8	teaspoon cayenne pepper
1	can (28 ounces) chopped tomatoes, with liquid
4	cups chicken broth
2	cups water
1	package (16 ounces) frozen corn kernels
1/2	cup all-purpose flour
2	cups whole milk
4	limes (2 quartered, 2 sliced)
1	cup chopped fresh cilantro leaves (for garnish)
1	cup shredded Manchego, Monterey Jack, or white cheddar cheese (for garnish)
2	cups tortilla chips or strips (for garnish)

MAKES 8 SERVINGS

In a large stockpot, heat oil and sauté onion until soft, about 4 to 5 minutes. Add garlic and chicken. Cook for 5 minutes, stirring often, to brown chicken on all sides. Add jalapeño peppers, chili powder, cumin, coriander, salt, pepper, cayenne pepper, tomatoes, broth, water, and corn. Cover; simmer for 30 minutes.

In a small bowl, whisk flour and milk until smooth. Slowly whisk into the soup, stirring for 1 to 2 minutes until well incorporated. Cook on low heat for 10 minutes, stirring often to prevent sticking on bottom. When ready to serve, squeeze a lime wedge into each serving bowl, sprinkle on cilantro, cheese, and tortilla strips, and top with a slice of lime.

Pumpkin Chipotle Soup with Pumpkin Seed Pesto

SOUP

- 2 tablespoons extra virgin olive oil
- 2 tablespoons butter
- 2 large shallots, minced
- 2 chipotle chiles in adobo (from a 7-ounce can), chopped
- 1 can (28 ounces) pumpkin puree
- 1 teaspoon ground cumin
- 6 cups chicken or vegetable broth
- 2 teaspoons kosher salt
- 1 cup sour cream

PUMPKIN SEED PESTO

- 1 cup fresh cilantro leaves
- Juice of 2 limes
- ¼ cup vegetable or canola oil
- ¼ cup extra virgin olive oil
- ½ cup toasted pumpkin seeds, shelled*
- 2 cloves garlic, coarsely chopped
- 1 teaspoon kosher salt

MAKES 4 SERVINGS

In a medium saucepan, heat oil and butter; sauté shallots until soft, about 2 minutes. Stir in chipotle chiles, pumpkin, cumin, broth, and salt. Stir, cover, and simmer for 20 minutes. Taste for seasoning. Remove from heat, stir in sour cream and serve with a dollop of pumpkin seed pesto on top.

Place all ingredients for pesto in the bowl of a food processor or in a blender. Puree until well combined, but not necessarily smooth. The pesto should have a somewhat coarse texture.

NOTE: This soup stores well in freezer.

*These are called pepitas in Mexican markets.

Shrimp and Leek Bisque

5   tablespoons butter, divided
1   pound raw shrimp, peeled and deveined, tails removed
1   leek, white part only, cleaned and finely chopped
2   tablespoons chopped fresh basil or 2 teaspoons dried basil leaves
Zest of 1 lemon
1   cup white wine
½   cup sherry or Madeira
24   ounces (3 8-ounce bottles) clam juice
¼   cup long grain rice
4   tablespoons tomato paste
2   cups half-and-half
    Pinch cayenne pepper
1   teaspoon kosher salt
¼   teaspoon ground black pepper
¼   cup chopped fresh chives (for garnish)

MAKES 6 SERVINGS

In a medium saucepan, heat 2 tablespoons butter. Add shrimp and sauté over medium heat until pink. Remove from pan; reserve 6 shrimp for garnish.

In the same pan, heat remaining butter. Sauté leeks until soft, about 2 minutes. Add basil, lemon zest, wine, sherry or Madeira, clam juice, rice, tomato paste, half-and-half, cayenne pepper, salt, and pepper. Cover and simmer for 20 minutes until rice is cooked through. Allow to cool slightly, then transfer to food processor in batches along with shrimp (except the reserved 6 shrimp.) Puree until smooth. Soup can be made ahead up to this point, then refrigerated.

Return pureed soup to saucepan and reheat on low. Taste for seasoning. Ladle into 6 soup bowls, place one shrimp in each bowl, sprinkle with chives, and serve at once.

Tortellini in Broth with Miniature Meatballs

TORTELLINI IN BROTH

2   tablespoons olive oil
2   tablespoons butter
1   small onion, chopped
2   carrots, peeled and chopped
2   ribs celery, chopped
2   cloves garlic, minced
1/8   teaspoon red pepper flakes
8   cups chicken or vegetable broth
1   recipe Miniature Meatballs
1   pound tortellini with cheese
4   cups fresh spinach leaves
1/2   cup chopped fresh basil leaves
1/2   cup grated Parmesan cheese (for garnish)
2   tomatoes, finely chopped (for garnish)

MINIATURE MEATBALLS

1   pound lean ground beef
1   large egg
1   cup dry bread crumbs
1   teaspoon kosher salt
1/4   teaspoon ground black pepper
1   clove garlic, minced
1   tablespoon Italian seasoning
1/4   cup chopped Italian parsley

MAKES 4 TO 6 SERVINGS

In a large stockpot, heat oil and butter. Sauté onion, carrots, and celery for 3 to 4 minutes over medium heat. Add garlic and red pepper flakes. Stir; cook 1 minute more. Add broth, bring to a boil, and then add the raw meatballs. Cover; reduce heat to a simmer for 20 minutes. Add tortellini, spinach, and basil. Cook for 5 minutes (tortellini should be floating to the surface at this point). Serve in large soup bowls with grated cheese and chopped tomatoes on top.

Mix all ingredients for Miniature Meatballs in a bowl until well combined. Form 1-inch balls and place on a platter until ready to add to soup. Makes about 20 miniature meatballs.

Vegetables

Eggplant, Squash, and Tomato Napoleons

2 tablespoons olive oil

1 large eggplant, cut across into ½-inch thick slices (8 slices total)

1 large or 2 medium zucchini, cut into ½-inch thick slices on diagonal (8 slices total)

1 large or 2 medium yellow squash, cut into ½-inch thick slices on diagonal (8 slices total)

Extra virgin olive oil

1 tablespoon kosher salt

1 teaspoon ground black pepper

2 large tomatoes, each cut into 4 slices, horizontally

¼ cup chopped mixed fresh herbs (such as basil, parsley, chervil, oregano, sage, and rosemary)

2 ounces feta cheese

4 sprigs (5-inch) fresh rosemary*

MAKES 4 SERVINGS

Brush a baking sheet with 1 tablespoon olive oil. Place eggplant slices on baking sheet; brush tops with another tablespoon olive oil. Bake at 400 degrees F for 10 minutes. Turn eggplant and add zucchini and yellow squash to pan; brush with more oil and sprinkle with salt and pepper. Bake for another 8 minutes.

To assemble napoleons, place a slice of eggplant on a work surface, top with a tomato slice, some of the chopped herbs, a zucchini slice, and a yellow squash slice. Repeat the layers in the same order to finish napoleon. Repeat this process until all the ingredients are used. You should have 4 stacks of vegetables using two eggplant, two tomato, two zucchini, and two yellow squash slices per stack. Sprinkle each napolean with feta cheese and secure the napoleon with a sprig of fresh rosemary placed through center. Serve warm. If you want to assemble ahead of time, don't add the feta cheese until you are ready to serve. Refrigerate the vegetable stacks and then reheat in at 350 degrees F for 5 minutes just before serving, and then add feta cheese.

*Remove all but the top 1 inch of herb from sprig and use in the chopped mixed fresh herbs.

Eggplant, Squash, and Tomato Napoleons

Asparagus Cheese Timbale

3　large eggs
1　cup half-and-half
2　cups ½-inch asparagus spears,
　　blanched for 2 minutes in simmering
　　water, and slightly cooled
4　ounces diced triple crème cheese
　　(such as St. Andre) or a rich brie or
　　camembert
1　teaspoon kosher salt
⅛　teaspoon ground white pepper
3　strips bacon, cooked and chopped
2　green onions, thinly sliced on
　　diagonal

MAKES 4 SERVINGS

In a medium bowl, whisk eggs with half-and-half. Stir in blanched asparagus, cheese, salt, pepper, bacon, and green onions. Butter four 1-cup ramekins. Divide the mixture evenly into each ramekin; place ramekins in a baking dish large enough to hold them, pour hot water half way up the sides of the ramekins, and bake in a preheated oven at 350 degrees F for 45 minutes. Remove from oven, cool slightly, and then serve the timbales unmolded.

Chive and Horseradish Smashed Potatoes

3　pounds white new potatoes
½　cup butter
1　tablespoon prepared horseradish
2　teaspoons kosher salt
½　teaspoon white pepper
1　cup sour cream
1 to 1½ cups half-and-half
¼　cup chopped fresh chives

MAKES 4 TO 6 SERVINGS

In a saucepot, bring potatoes to a boil in enough water to cover. Lower heat to a simmer and cook until tender, about 15 to 20 minutes. Drain.

In a bowl, place potatoes, butter, horseradish, salt, and pepper. With a potato masher, mash until potatoes are softened and butter is incorporated. Stir in sour cream, half-and-half, and chives. Taste for seasoning. Place in a prepared baking dish and heat at 350 degrees F for 15 minutes just before serving. This recipe can be made a day ahead. (You might have to heat the dish a little longer if the potatoes are cold.)

Eggplant Caviar with Pita Chips

EGGPLANT CAVIAR

2 large eggplants, cut in half lengthwise

6 whole cloves garlic, peeled

½ cup tahini (sesame seed paste)
Juice of 2 lemons

⅛ teaspoon cayenne pepper or 1 teaspoon Tabasco sauce

1 teaspoon kosher salt

3 tablespoons olive oil

2 tablespoons chopped fresh cilantro

1 large tomato, chopped (about ½ cup)

PITA CHIPS

6 pita bread rounds, each cut into 8 wedges
Vegetable or olive oil spray

MAKES 4 TO 6 SERVINGS

Place eggplant, cut side down, and garlic on a baking sheet lined with parchment paper. Bake at 375 degrees F for 40 minutes until eggplant is soft. Cool until ready to handle. In food processor, place the pulp scraped out of the eggplant, garlic, tahini, lemon juice, cayenne pepper or Tabasco sauce, salt, olive oil, cilantro, and tomato in a food processor. Pulse on and off until finely chopped, not pureed. Taste for seasoning.

Place the pita bread triangles on a baking sheet in a single layer and spray lightly with vegetable or olive oil spray. Bake for 10 minutes at 375 degrees F.

Place eggplant "caviar" in a serving bowl; place pita triangles around eggplant for dipping.

Grilled Leeks and Asparagus with Confetti Vinaigrette

Grilled Leeks and Asparagus with Confetti Vinaigrette

LEEKS AND ASPARAGUS

2 large leeks, trimmed to about 6 inches of the white end
20 stalks asparagus, trimmed to 6-inch lengths
Olive oil for grilling

CONFETTI VINAIGRETTE

1 tablespoon Dijon mustard
¼ cup white wine vinegar
½ cup olive oil
1 clove garlic, minced
½ teaspoon kosher salt
¼ cup chopped mixed herbs (such as basil, chives, parsley, mint, tarragon, and thyme)
¼ cup finely chopped red bell peppers
¼ cup finely chopped yellow bell peppers
¼ cup diced kalamata olives

MAKES 4 SERVINGS

Cut leeks into quarters lengthwise. You will have 8 quarters. Rinse each quarter well. With kitchen string, tie 5 asparagus spears and 2 leek quarters together. Blanch vegetables in boiling salted water for 2 minutes. Drain on paper towels. The recipe can be made ahead up to this point.

Heat an outdoor grill to medium. Brush vegetable bundles with oil and grill for 3 to 4 minutes per side (for a total of 6 to 8 minutes cooking time) or until leeks are golden and asparagus is heated through. Place on serving platters, remove string, and spoon some vinaigrette on each.

To make Confetti Vinaigrette, whisk together mustard, vinegar, oil, garlic, salt, and herbs in a medium bowl. Stir in bell peppers and olives after whisking.

Haricots Verts and Tomatoes

1½ to 2 pounds haricots verts*
  (trimmed, if fresh or thawed, if
  frozen)
4 cups water
1 tablespoon extra virgin olive oil
2 teaspoons kosher salt
4 large tomatoes, chopped
½ cup kalamata olives, coarsely
  chopped
1 teaspoon capers
1 small red onion, thinly sliced
2 large cloves garlic, minced
½ cup chopped fresh Italian parsley
½ cup extra virgin olive oil
3 tablespoons wine vinegar
1 teaspoon kosher salt
½ teaspoon ground black pepper

MAKES 6 SERVINGS

Bring water to a boil with 1 tablespoon olive oil and salt. Cook beans in salted water for 3 minutes; drain and cool. In a mixing bowl, combine tomatoes, olives, capers, red onion, garlic, parsley, olive oil, vinegar, salt, and pepper. Add the cooled green beans, toss, and refrigerate until ready to serve.

NOTE: Frozen petite green beans or haricots verts are now available in markets and are a great buy. Using frozen beans gives the added bonus of not having to clean them.

*French green beans.

Haricots Verts and Tomatoes

Oven-Roasted Cauliflower and Tomatoes with Blue Cheese Crumbs

CAULIFLOWER AND TOMATOES

- 1 large head cauliflower, cored and cut into florets
- 1/4 cup extra virgin olive oil
- 1 tablespoon kosher salt
- 1 teaspoon coarse ground black pepper
- 2 large cloves garlic, minced
- 4 Roma tomatoes, cored and cut in half lengthwise

BLUE CHEESE CRUMB TOPPING

- 2 tablespoons butter
- 2 tablespoons olive oil
- 1 large clove garlic, minced
- 1 cup bread crumbs*
- 1 teaspoon dried Italian seasoning
- 1/2 cup crumbled blue cheese
- 1/4 cup chopped fresh basil leaves (for garnish)

MAKES 4 SERVINGS

In a medium mixing bowl, toss cauliflower with oil, salt, pepper, and garlic. Place cauliflower in a single layer on a baking sheet, leaving some of the oil in bowl. Toss the tomatoes in the remaining oil mixture, then arrange around the cauliflower, cut side up. Roast in a preheated oven at 400 degrees F for 15 minutes, until cauliflower is golden brown.

To make topping, heat butter and oil in a medium skillet. Sauté garlic for 30 seconds over medium heat, then add bread crumbs and Italian seasoning. Cook for 1 minute, so crumbs are evenly golden brown. Remove pan from heat; stir in the blue cheese. Place the cauliflower and tomatoes on a serving platter, sprinkle with the blue cheese crumb topping, and garnish with the fresh basil leaves. Serve at once.

*I like using soft bread crumbs made from day old bread.

Grilled Summer Vegetables

1   bunch asparagus, ends trimmed, cut into 2-inch pieces
2   zucchini, cut into 1-inch pieces
2   yellow squash, cut into 1-inch pieces
1   red bell pepper, cored and cut into 1-inch pieces
1   yellow bell pepper, cored and cut into 1-inch pieces
1   pound baby new potatoes, cut in half and parboiled for 5 to 7 minutes
1   red onion, thinly sliced
¼   cup olive oil
2   cloves garlic, thinly sliced
¼   cup mixed chopped fresh herbs (such as parsley, thyme, rosemary, basil)
2   teaspoons kosher salt
½   teaspoon coarse ground black pepper

MAKES 6 TO 8 SERVINGS

Place all ingredients in a bowl and toss. Place vegetables in a basket on an outdoor grill and cook over medium heat until tender, about 10 minutes. Toss the basket often to allow the heat to evenly cook the vegetables.

Sicilian Swiss Chard, Pancetta, and Beans

1 tablespoon extra virgin olive oil

¼ pound pancetta or bacon, thinly sliced and cut into thin strips

½ cup diced onion

2 large cloves garlic, minced

1 teaspoon dried oregano

⅛ teaspoon red pepper flakes

2 bunches Swiss chard (red, white, or rainbow), washed, tough ends removed, coarsely chopped

1 can (15 ounces) cannellini or Great Northern White beans, drained and rinsed

2 large tomatoes, chopped

¼ cup golden raisins

¼ cup toasted pine nuts

¼ cup grated Romano or Parmesan cheese

MAKES 4 SERVINGS

In a large skillet, heat oil and sauté pancetta or bacon until lightly browned. Add onion, garlic, oregano, and red pepper flakes. Cook for 2 minutes. Add chard, beans, tomatoes, raisins, and pine nuts. Cover skillet and simmer over low heat for 5 minutes, stirring often. Chard should be wilted at this point. Taste for seasoning. Serve with grated cheese sprinkled on top.

NOTE: This vegetable dish makes a simple, colorful base for grilled chicken, sliced steak, or a piece of fish such as halibut or snapper. It has flavors of Sicily with the addition of raisins and pine nuts. This can also be served with imported pasta of your choice, preferably a short tubular shaped pasta, from Italy, of course.

Sicilian Swiss Chard, Pancetta, and Beans

Pearl Onions and Wild Mushroom Au Gratin

4   large portobello mushrooms, stems removed
2   tablespoons butter
2   tablespoons olive oil
2   shallots, minced
1   teaspoon dried thyme
1   teaspoon kosher salt
¼   teaspoon ground white or black pepper
½   teaspoon paprika
1   bag (16 ounces) frozen whole pearl onions, thawed
1   cup heavy cream
2   cups fresh bread crumbs
¼   cup olive oil
2   cups grated Swiss cheese
½   cup finely chopped Italian parsley

MAKES 6 TO 8 SERVINGS

Thinly slice the mushrooms and set aside. In a large skillet, heat butter and oil. Sauté shallots and thyme for 1 to 2 minutes. Add mushrooms; cook for 3 minutes, stirring often. Add salt, pepper, paprika, onions, and cream. Simmer over low heat for 3 to 4 minutes until onions are cooked and sauce has thickened slightly. Pour into a shallow au gratin dish.

In a small bowl, combine bread crumbs, oil, cheese, and parsley. Sprinkle evenly over the mushroom mixture. The recipe can be made several hours ahead up to this point. Bake in preheated oven at 375 degrees F for 15 minutes until cheese is melted and filling is bubbly.

Three-Cheese Stuffed Mushrooms on Tomato Couscous

MUSHROOM MIXTURE

4	large portobello mushrooms (about 5 inches in diameter) or 8 portobellini mushrooms (about 3-inch in diameter)
4	tablespoons olive oil
1	tablespoon kosher salt

CHEESE FILLING

8	ounces ricotta cheese, drained
4	ounces mozzarella, cut into 1/2-inch dice
1	cup grated Romano, Asiago, or Parmesan cheese
$\frac{1}{4}$	cup chopped fresh basil leaves
1	teaspoon kosher salt
$\frac{1}{2}$	teaspoon ground black pepper
1	large egg, lightly beaten

TOMATO COUSCOUS

1	package plain instant couscous, cooked according to directions*
4	Roma tomatoes, finely chopped
$\frac{1}{2}$	cup chopped fresh basil leaves
1	large clove garlic, minced
1	teaspoon kosher salt
$\frac{1}{2}$	cup toasted pine nuts
$\frac{1}{2}$	cup chopped fresh parsley (for garnish)

MAKES 4 SERVINGS

Remove the stems from mushrooms. Clean mushrooms with damp paper towel to wipe off excess dirt, if necessary. Brush the top and bottom of each mushroom with olive oil. Place mushroom caps on a baking sheet, "gill" side up, and sprinkle each with kosher salt.

In a medium bowl, combine all ingredients for cheese filling, mixing well. Divide the mixture among the mushrooms. This can be done several hours ahead and refrigerated. Bake filled mushrooms in a preheated oven at 350 degrees F for 25 to 30 minutes until cheese is bubbly and mushrooms are cooked through.

In a medium bowl, combine cooked couscous, tomatoes, basil, garlic, salt, and pine nuts. Spread the couscous mixture out on a serving platter, top with the baked and stuffed mushrooms, and sprinkle on the chopped parsley for garnish.

*Near East brand is good.

Wild Mushrooms on Creamy Polenta

MUSHROOM MIXTURE

2   tablespoons olive oil
2   tablespoons butter
2   large shallots, finely chopped
4   cups mixed fresh wild mushrooms, sliced*
1   teaspoon dried thyme leaves
1   cup red wine
½   teaspoon kosher salt
¼   teaspoon ground black pepper

CREAMY POLENTA

6   cups water or chicken broth
2   cups polenta (Italian cornmeal)
1   tablespoon kosher salt
2   tablespoons butter
½   cup heavy cream
¼   cup grated Romano cheese (for garnish)
Fresh thyme sprigs (for garnish)

MAKES 4 TO 6 SERVINGS

Heat a medium sauté pan and add oil and butter. Add shallots, mushrooms, and thyme; cook 5 minutes. Add wine, salt, and pepper and cook another 3 minutes until thickened slightly.

Bring water or broth to a boil and slowly whisk in the polenta and salt. Slowly stir until combined; cook over low heat, stirring often, for 10 to 15 minutes until thickened and polenta is no longer coarse. Stir in butter and cream; cook another minute. Place a cupful of polenta on each plate and top with some of the mushroom mixture. Garnish with cheese and fresh thyme leaves.

*Or you can use 1/4 cup dried mushrooms, rehydrated, plus 1/2 pound fresh mushrooms of choice such as portobello, oyster, chanterelles, crimini, or shiitake.

Wild Mushrooms on Creamy Polenta

Warm Mozzarella and Tomato Stacks

TOASTED BREAD ROUNDS

1   French baguette, cut into 1/2-inch thick slices, about 16 slices

Olive oil

VINAIGRETTE

2   cloves garlic, minced
1/3   cup balsamic vinegar
2/3   cup olive oil
2   shallots, minced
1   tablespoon capers
1   teaspoon kosher salt
1/4   teaspoon coarse ground black pepper
1/2   cup pitted kalamata olives, chopped
1/2   cup fresh basil leaves

MOZZARELLA AND TOMATOES

8   large Roma tomatoes
1   pound fresh mozzarella, cut into 16 slices

MAKES 16 SERVINGS

Place baguette slices on a baking sheet and brush with olive oil. Place under broiler for 2 minutes until golden brown. Place toasted baguette slices in a single layer on a serving platter.

In a bowl, combine garlic, vinegar, oil, shallots, capers, salt, pepper, olives, and basil. Whisk well.

Slice each of the tomatoes into 4 slices lengthwise, to make 32 slices. Place one slice tomato in large baking dish, top with one slice mozzarella, then another slice tomato; drizzle with some of the vinaigrette. Repeat until all of the tomato and mozzarella slices have been used. Recipe can be made an hour ahead up to this point. Place baking dish in a preheated oven at 400 degrees F for 8 to 10 minutes, until cheese is melted. Remove from oven and place one tomato stack on each toasted bread round.

Parslied Potatoes and Parsnips Parmesan

3   pounds russet potatoes, peeled and cut into 1-inch pieces
4   small or 2 large parsnips, peeled and cut into 1-inch pieces
4   quarts water
1   tablespoon kosher salt
1/2   cup butter
2   cups half-and-half
1/4   teaspoon ground nutmeg
2   cups grated Parmesan cheese
1   cup chopped fresh Italian parsley
1   teaspoon kosher salt

Pinch cayenne pepper

MAKES 6 TO 8 SERVINGS

Boil potatoes and parsnips in water with 1 tablespoon salt added until potatoes are tender. Drain. In a mixer (do not use a processor), place the hot potatoes and parsnips along with butter, half-and-half, nutmeg, Parmesan, parsley, salt, and cayenne pepper. On low speed, beat the mixture with the paddle attachment until blended and smooth. Taste for seasoning. Pour into a serving dish to serve immediately. If you are making the recipe ahead of time, pour it into an ovenproof dish, then reheat later in a preheated oven at 350 degrees F for 15 to 20 minutes, uncovered.

Oven-Roasted Autumn Vegetables

1½ to 2 pounds yams or sweet potatoes, peeled and cut into 1-inch cubes

1½ to 2 pounds banana or Hubbard squash, peeled and cut into 1-inch cubes

1 pound Brussels sprouts, ends trimmed and cut into halves

2 large carrots, peeled and cut into 1/2-inch thick slices

1 red onion, thinly sliced

2 parsnips, peeled and cut into 1/2-inch thick slices

1 medium head cauliflower, cored and cut into florets

4 large cloves garlic, smashed

2 teaspoons dried thyme leaves

¼ cup extra virgin olive oil

1 tablespoon kosher salt

1 teaspoon ground black pepper

½ cup chopped Italian parsley (for garnish)

MAKES 6 TO 8 SERVINGS

In a large mixing bowl, combine all the ingredients except for the parsley. Toss well. Spread out on a baking sheet lined with parchment paper. Roast in preheated oven at 375 degrees F for 20 to 25 minutes until yams and carrots are tender (they take the longest to cook). Place in a serving bowl, top with parsley, and serve warm.

NOTE: For easy preparation, cut all the vegetables the day before roasting and store in individual zipper-lock bags until ready to use.

Index

Boldface numbers indicate a photograph.